WEAPON

THE SPATHA

M.C. BISHOP
Series Editor Martin Pegler

Illustrated by Peter Dennis

OSPREY PUBLISHING
Bloomsbury Publishing Plc

Kemp House, Chawley Park, Oxford OX2 9PH, UK
29 Earlsfort Terrace, Dublin 2, Ireland
1385 Broadway, 5th Floor, New York, NY 10018, USA
Email: info@ospreypublishing.com
www.ospreypublishing.com

OSPREY is a trademark of Osprey Publishing Ltd

First published in Great Britain in 2020
Transferred to digital print in 2024

A catalogue record for this book is available from the British Library.

Print ISBN: 978 1 4728 3239 9
ePub: 978 1 4728 3240 5
ePDF: 978 1 4728 3238 2
XML: 978 1 4728 3241 2

Index by Rob Munro
Typeset by PDQ Digital Media Solutions, Bungay, UK
Printed and bound in Great Britain by CPI (Group) UK Ltd, Croydon CR0 4YY

24 25 26 27 28   10 9 8 7 6 5 4 3 2

The Woodland Trust
Osprey Publishing supports the Woodland Trust, the UK's leading woodland conservation charity.

www.ospreypublishing.com
To find out more about our authors and books visit our website. Here you will find extracts, author interviews, details of forthcoming events and the option to sign-up for our newsletter.

Acknowledgements

As ever, I am grateful to a number of individuals who have helped me in preparing this volume. I am indebted to Erik Graafstal, Holger von Grawert, Matt Lukes, Professor Dr Günther Moosbauer, Martina Meyr, and Dr Ivan Radman-Livaja for helping source images; and Jon Coulston, Philip Gross, Róbert Môc, and Robert Wimmers for allowing me to use their photographs. The Ermine Street Guard were kind enough to allow me to photograph one of their replica *spathae*. Particular thanks are due to Dr David Sim, consummate blacksmith and wielder of sharp weapons, for his insights into all things swordsmithing, but not least fire welding, pattern welding, and damage and repair. He was also good enough to read and comment upon a draft of the text. Jon Coulston similarly very kindly read and commented upon an early version of the text. I am especially grateful to Barbara Birley and the Vindolanda Trust for allowing me to examine their swords at first hand and Frances McIntosh of English Heritage for enabling me to use a photograph of the Corbridge Hoard scabbard. While this book has certainly benefited from all of these contributions, all faults, errors and idiosyncrasies that remain are my sole responsibility.

Author's note

The text, captions, and table of dimensions include reference numbers for Miks' (2007) catalogue of Roman swords. Swords with no such number were not included in that publication, either because they were not deemed to be Roman or are recent discoveries.

Editor's note

Metric measurements are used in this book. For ease of comparison please refer to the following conversion table:

1m = 1.09yd / 3.28ft / 39.37in
1cm = 0.39in
1mm = 0.04in
1kg = 2.20lb
1g = 0.04oz

Cover illustrations are (top) © M.C. Bishop, and (bottom) © Osprey Publishing.
Title-page photograph: The tombstone of Insus, an *eques* from the *ala Augusta*, found at Lancaster (Lancashire, England), wielding both his *spatha* and the severed head of a defeated foe, whose naked, headless corpse is being trampled by the cavalryman's horse. (Photo © M.C. Bishop)

Artist's note

Readers may care to note that the original paintings from which the colour plates in this book were prepared are available for private sale. All reproduction copyright whatsoever is retained by the publishers. All enquiries should be addressed to:

Peter Dennis, 'Fieldhead', The Park, Mansfield, Nottinghamshire NG18 2AT, UK, or email magie.h@ntlworld.com

The publishers regret that they can enter into no correspondence upon this matter.

CONTENTS

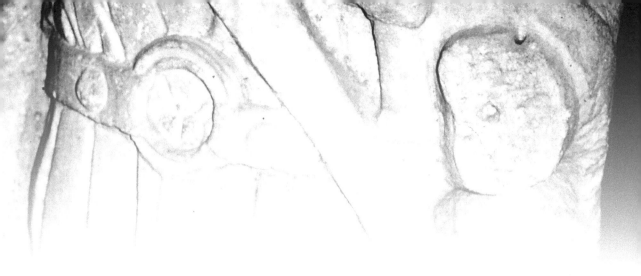

INTRODUCTION

In a well-known passage describing the Roman assault on a British stronghold, the historian Tacitus used a false dichotomy to make a clear distinction between legionary troops and auxiliary soldiers, but in doing so it can be argued that he was being economical with the truth: 'If they offered a resistance to the auxiliaries, they were struck down by the *gladii* and *pila* of the legionaries; if they faced against the legionaries, they fell under the *spathae* and *hastae* of the auxiliaries' (Tacitus, *Annals* 12.35).

There is plenty of evidence to show that auxiliary infantry at the time used the *gladius*, just like the legionaries, and that only cavalrymen used the longer *spatha*. The use of the word *spathae* is often cited as a 'mistake' by Tacitus, but it is an interesting one. This is the first time in the surviving Roman literary record that the word *spathae* is used to describe swords. We should perhaps also be careful about criticizing Tacitus' seemingly imprecise use of the word here. Taken in context, where he is describing the assault by Roman troops on a hilltop stronghold held by the British resistance leader Caratacus, and as at least one scholar has observed, the army commander Ostorius Scapula may have been using dismounted cavalry, who would of course have been using the longer *spatha*.

The auxiliary cavalry were the Roman Army's butchers and their habit of taking heads in battle only serves to reinforce this impression. Stationed on the wings in battle, their job was to let the infantry break an enemy and then, as they fled, to charge into their rear and inflict the greatest possible number of casualties to ensure they did not rally. This is why battle casualty figures – even allowing for the inevitable literary exaggeration – were so disproportionate between Romans and their barbarian foes. Equipped with javelins, a thrusting spear and the *spatha*, the cavalry also fulfilled scouting, skirmishing and communications roles, probably far more often than they participated in set-piece battles. The historian Arrian followed a Hellenistic tradition in naming such light cavalry Tarantine (meaning skirmishing, after Hellenistic light cavalry from Tarentum in Italy), but the senior *decurio* (troop commander) in a cavalry unit based at Carlisle (Cumbria, England) during the time of Hadrian referred to his men as *lanciarii* or 'javelineers'.

During the 2nd century AD, a particularly intriguing process can be identified, whereby the sword used by these cavalrymen began to be adopted by the infantry. Why this happened is one of the most interesting questions in the study of Roman weaponry, because it was a very clear and decisive move away from the traditional Roman infantry reliance upon the short sword. Conservatism is perhaps responsible for the appearance for a while of *semispathae* (mostly but not exclusively cut-down broken *spathae*), but the long sword won through.

At the same time, the *spatha* was to evolve in both form and technical competence. The introduction of pattern welding may have been intended to strengthen the core of the blade, while inlay with contrasting metals enhanced its appearance. Similarly, the use of forged fullers enabled strong, lightweight blades to be fashioned. New methods of casting copper alloys, particularly the adoption of the two-part mould – hundreds of years old but ignored by the Roman Army up until this point in favour of the lost wax method – meant that scabbard and baldric fittings could more easily be cast in larger numbers and even directly copied in the case of popular designs.

To some extent, it is understandable that the history of the Roman *spatha* has tended to be overshadowed by that of the short sword, usually known as the *gladius,* although that term was often used generally of all swords. In fact, the *spatha* underwent a complex and interesting evolution from an Iron Age long sword used by both Gallic infantry and cavalry, through a time as an exclusively auxiliary cavalry sidearm, until it came to equip all branches of the Roman Army, both infantry and cavalry (Bishop & Coulston 2006: 82; 130; 154–63; 202–05). As such, its versatility was remarkable, allowing it to adapt to changes in styles of fighting over several centuries. Indeed, it went from being mocked by the Romans to being the sword upon which the Roman Army depended. Moreover, its use was not limited to the duration of the Roman Empire. The direct influence of the Roman *spatha* can be seen in the weaponry of the early medieval or Migration period throughout north-western Europe, especially among Rome's Germanic and Norse neighbours. This was something that could not be claimed for its more glamorous sibling, the short sword.

It is important that, before venturing any further, the difference between the short sword, typified by the *gladius Hispaniensis* and its successors, and the *spatha* should be unambiguously defined. Unfortunately, that is by no means an easy task (Miks 2007: 77), and there is no guarantee that a modern definition is one that a Roman would recognize or even care about. Nevertheless, as a general rule, *spathae* tended to be between 540mm and 815mm in length, and 35mm and 65mm in width, while the short sword (or *gladius*) ranged between 430mm and 770mm in length, and 40mm and 75mm in width. It will be instantly apparent from the overlap that general rules are next to useless and archaeological context a much more reliable means of determining

The taking of heads by auxiliaries as depicted in Scene XXIV on Trajan's Column in Rome (Italy). (Photo © M.C. Bishop)

what kind of sword is being dealt with in any given instance. Dealing with handmade weapons from a pre-industrial age when even common measures could vary, this is hardly surprising, however unsatisfactory it may be. An example of such variety came to light when two *spathae* found together in a double grave within Canterbury-Durovernum (Kent, England) differed in length by 5 per cent.

Examples of *spatha* hilt types (in reality each period had many forms): (top row, left to right) Celtic, early Imperial Roman, later Imperial Roman, Dominate; (bottom row) Germanic, Saxon and Viking. (Drawings M.C. Bishop)

DEVELOPMENT
Changing function

By comparison with the *gladius*, far greater numbers of *spathae* have survived in the archaeological record – more than 600 blades – mainly due to the examples found in watery (and usually votive) contexts in Northern Europe. Many of these are extremely well preserved, allowing the recovery of data about size and weight that might not be retrievable for other excavated examples. It is worth noting that there is more than one typological system for sword types, ranging from Ulbert's (1974) simple view through to the complex types and variants of Biborski (1993), Biborski & Ilkjaer (2006) and Miks (2007). What follows is inevitably an attempt to reach a compromise between these various classifications.

GALLIC/CELTIC ORIGINS
When Gallic troops first started to serve with the Roman Army as allied troops during the Second Punic War (218–201 BC), they would have used their own, native weaponry and equipment. This would naturally have included the sort of long swords recovered archaeologically from the 3rd and 2nd centuries BC. Roman records of such swords verged on the contemptuous:

> Finally, when Camillus led his men into the attack, the enemy raised their swords and rushed into close quarters. However, the Romans thrust their javelins into their faces, parried their blows on the iron-clad parts, and so turned the edge of their blade, which was soft and weakly tempered, so much so that their swords soon bent in two ...
> (Plutarch, *Camillus* 41.4)

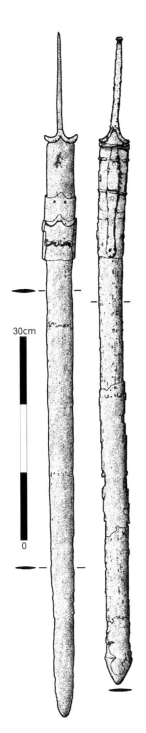

This passage was written some six centuries after the events it describes, and that fact neatly highlights one of the problems with accepting such accounts without question. This is not the only description of the limited capabilities of Gallic swords, however. Referring to the Celtiberian troops at the battle of Cannae in 216 BC, the historian Polybius (writing less than a century after the events he was describing) noted that 'The shields of the Spaniards and Celts were very similar, but their swords were entirely different, those of the Spaniards thrusting with deadly effect when they cut, but the Gallic sword was only able to slash and requiring a long swing to do so' (Polybius, *Histories* 3.114).

The shortcomings of at least some of the Gallic blades were therefore well known, although the structural weaknesses do not seem to have been universal. Philo of Byzantium, writing about artillery in the 3rd century BC, permitted himself an aside in which he described a test that steel swords were subjected to:

> The production of the above-mentioned strips can be seen with the so-called Celtic and Spanish swords. For if they are to be tested for utility, one grips the handle with the right hand, the tip of the sword with the other, places it across the head, and pulls it down on both sides until the shoulders are touched. Then both hands are released by withdrawing them rapidly, but the sword, let loose, straighten itself again, and returns to its former shape, so that it no longer has any hint of curvature. Even if performed repeatedly, they remain straight. (Philon, *Belopoeica* 71.10–20)

If the origin of the Roman *spatha* lay principally with the Gallic, Celtiberian and other 'Celtic' blades of Western Europe, there is at least a possibility that Germanic weapons may have been influential. The overlap between Gallic and Germanic culture in the 1st millennium BC is still debated by scholars and there was clearly cross-fertilization of ideas and technology. Tacitus (*Germania* 6.1) describes how, while most tribes preferred to fight with the stabbing spear, some happily fought with the sword and javelins. The Batavi, generally accepted by modern scholars as having been transplanted from the right bank of the Rhine into Roman territory around modern-day Nijmegen in the Netherlands, were to go on to provide some of the most notable of Roman auxiliary cavalry, as well as the early emperors' personal bodyguard, the *Germani corporis custodes*.

The short sword also had its part to play in the development of the *spatha*. The original *gladius Hispaniensis* was much longer than the equivalent blades of the early Principate period and was used by both infantry and cavalry: a description of the lethal effects of the weapon (Livy, *History of Rome* 31.34.4; see Bishop 2016a: 4) in fact refers to its use by Roman cavalry.

In the Augustan period, the length of the new 'Mainz-type' *gladius* blade was noticeably reduced from that of the earlier, dual-purpose *gladius Hispaniensis*, which meant that the new shorter sword did not have adequate reach for mounted troops. A new type of cavalry sword was therefore needed. The employment of Gallic or 'Celtic' cavalry by

Two late La Tène swords from France of the type that Gallic auxiliary cavalry might have used. It is among these 1st-century BC weapons that the *spatha* has its origins. (Drawings M.C. Bishop)

30cm

0

both the Romans and Carthaginians during the Second Punic War saw the origin of what, by the early Principate period, would be known as auxiliary cavalry in Roman service. It was probably these men who introduced the longer, parallel-edged sword that would be the prototype for the *spatha*.

LATE REPUBLICAN

The earliest examples of the *spatha* in Roman service were in fact simply native swords and cannot really be described as Roman at all. This means it is virtually impossible to distinguish those blades belonging to those that fought for the Romans from those that were used against them, a dilemma typified by the finds from the siege site of Alesia (Alise-Sainte-Reine, France) in 52 BC (Rapin 2001).

The earliest blades have been categorized into two principal types by Miks (2007: 77–80), namely the 'Fontillet' and 'Nauportus' forms. Many of these, however, can probably be classified as *gladii*, strictly speaking, because the Republican *gladii* were so much larger than their successors. The key to distinguishing the *spatha*-type blades from derivatives of the *gladius Hispaniensis* therefore lies in the form and proportions of the sword.

EARLY PRINCIPATE

The first cavalry units serving under Augustus as auxiliaries were natives brought into the Roman Army, still armed with their own weaponry. Roman examples of such native-type *spathae* are just as difficult to isolate as their immediate forebears, because they obviously closely resembled the native originals. Nevertheless, it is possible to identify some burials where such weapons were included, particularly because the earliest recruits to the cavalry retained their native burial customs for a while. A fragmentary blade was found at Chassenard (France) in the tomb of an individual who may have commanded such an early Principate auxiliary unit during the first half of the 1st century AD. The presence of a cavalry face-mask helmet in the tomb suggests that the sword, 45mm wide and only surviving to 164mm in length, may have been one of these early weapons.

An enigmatic statue from Vachères (France), long thought to depict a Gallic warrior, may in fact show a very early Principate cavalryman in the service of Rome, with the same mail shirt worn over a long-sleeved tunic with broad cuffs found on auxiliary cavalry tombstones of the 1st century AD. His sword is recognizably of a native type and it has been suggested that just such a weapon exists today in a private collection. This 'proto-*spatha*', with a gently tapering blade with no discernible point, is still in its sheath, which is decorated with an embossed brass locket plate which portrays mythical beasts, human figures and a horseman (Miks 2015).

Unprovenanced early 'proto-*spatha*'-type sword with an embossed brass locket plate now in a private collection. (Photo P. Gross © Arachne)

9

Most Roman cavalry tombstones of the 1st century AD depict riders carrying spears or javelins and with sheathed swords, but there is a rather unusual exception to this. The tombstone of Insus (see page 1) from Lancaster (Lancashire, England) depicts a cavalryman who served in the *ala Augusta* when it was based at the fort there. He holds his oval shield in his left hand, but in his right hand he brandishes not only his sword but also the decapitated head of his foe, the headless corpse of whom is being trampled by his horse. The sword is shown with a very pronounced point and bears more than a passing resemblance to an infantry *gladius*. However, the observer is left in little doubt that it is the edge of the blade that has just seen use. Head-taking by auxiliary soldiers is also depicted on Trajan's Column in Rome (Italy), so should occasion no surprise, but its depiction on a tombstone is rare and a clear testament to the efficacy of the weapon.

During the final quarter of the 1st century AD, in the Flavian period, the influence of the 'Pompeii-type' short sword becomes most marked in surviving examples of what, for obvious reasons (parallel-edged blade and short triangular point), was effectively a Pompeii-type *spatha* (termed the 'Newstead type' by Miks). It is probably this form of the weapon that was being intended on Insus' tombstone.

The campaigns of the Roman general Gnaeus Iulius Agricola (the historian Tacitus' father-in-law) in what is now Scotland saw the foundation of the Flavian fort at Newstead-Trimontium (Scottish Borders). A diligent campaign of archaeological excavations at the beginning of the 20th century produced numerous archaeological examples of weaponry and other military equipment from the site, many in an excellent state of preservation. These finds included two definite examples of *spatha* blades (Miks A526–27) from pits in the southern annexe of the fort. Both blades were much narrower than those of Pompeii-type short swords and had diamond cross-sections, one of them with a more pronounced point. That these two contemporary swords from the same site are so similar is scarcely surprising; and their narrowness shows that the Pompeii-type *spatha* was not simply an elongated version of the short sword.

The Newstead swords are matched by an example from the Rhine at Mainz in Germany (Miks A468), virtually identical in blade length but with a longer tang, still retaining its top nut. Another such sword occurred as an isolated find from Falkirk (Stirlingshire, Scotland), and is also probably Flavian in date (Miks A94). This, however, was both longer and broader than the contemporary Newstead examples.

A similarly proportioned *spatha* blade excavated from a Flavian context at Rottweil in Germany (Miks A617), like the Mainz and Falkirk

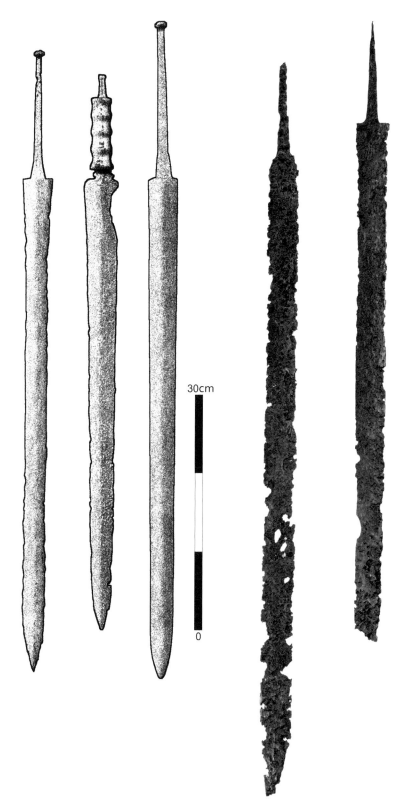

30cm

0

FAR LEFT
Pompeii-type *spathae* from (left to right) Diersheim (Miks A125; Germany), Alem (Miks A7; Netherlands) and Mainz (Miks A468; Germany). (Drawings M.C. Bishop)

LEFT
Two *spathae* (Miks A617–18) from Rottweil (Germany) of the Straubing (left) and Newstead (right) types. (Photo Luca Hoffmannbeck, Hak Design © Städtische Museen Rottweil)

swords, differs from the Newstead blades in having a lenticular cross-section. A sword dating to the last quarter of the 1st century AD from a burial at Diersheim (Germany) had a longer tang but slightly shorter blade and retained its top nut and a fragment of its bone hand grip (Miks A125).

The eruption of Mount Vesuvius in AD 79 famously buried several examples of the *gladius* in Pompeii (Italy) and other Bay of Naples sites, and two round-shouldered *spathae* in the collection of the National Archaeological Museum in Naples have been suggested as coming from the area, although there is a possibility that they actually originate from another Italian site some distance away, at Pietrabbondante (Ortisi 2015: 17–18, 119).

One of several sword finds made close together, a lenticular-sectioned *spatha* from Vindolanda (Northumberland, England) was discovered within a cavalry stable-barrack and, although lacking its tip, retained wooden laths from its scabbard. The wooden pommel and part of the hand grip also survived, but the hand guard and top nut were missing. A second, lenticular-sectioned sword found nearby was broken across the blade and seemed to have been in the process of being reworked before being discarded. The unit in garrison was a *cohors equitata*, which helps explain why a third sword found was a classic Pompeii-type *gladius*, because such units contained both infantry and cavalry.

The collection of artefacts buried in a chest during the early 2nd century AD and known as the Corbridge Hoard (excavated from within the fort at Corbridge in Northumberland, England) included a scabbard which was designed to hold a *spatha*-type sword (Allason-Jones & Bishop 1988: 75, Fig. 93). The sheath (see page 10) was made from a single piece of copper-alloy sheet, folded over on itself and riveted together with a medial strip, and lacked a chape. The blade itself was not present, but the dimensions of the sheath suggest it was up to 700mm long and tapered from around 65mm to 25mm in width over its length. A tombstone from nearby in Hexham, belonging to the standard-bearer Flavinus of the *ala Petriana*, has been associated with the late 1st/early 2nd century AD cavalry garrison of Corbridge (the Roman town was used as a source of stone for building Hexham Abbey), which may explain the presence of this scabbard in the chest.

An elaborate burial from Tell Oum Hauran, just outside Nawa in Syria, appears to have been that of a local member of the nobility who had served with the Roman Army, perhaps as the commanding officer of an auxiliary *ala*. The deceased embarked upon the afterlife equipped with both a sports and battle helmet, armour, horse harness, spears, two daggers, and both a short sword and a long sword (with a total length of 710mm). The published details of the long sword are sparse, but from its length it was clearly a *spatha*, while the limited dating evidence suggests that the burial belonged to the first half of the 2nd century AD.

Where actual examples survive, hand guards of this early form of *spatha* were often decorated with an incised, inverted-V-shaped design, a feature which is depicted on a number of cavalry swords in Scene XXXVII on Trajan's Column. These motifs are never found on the many *in situ*

0   10cm

gladius hand guards and thus seem to have been a characteristic of the Pompeii-type *spatha*.

One of the latest examples of the early Principate cavalry *spatha* comes from Iža (Slovakia) from deposits associated with the Marcomannic Wars (AD 166–180). As the shorter *gladius*-type sword was also present at the site, that too was clearly still in use. By this time, Sarmatian-influenced ring-pommel swords were also (briefly) in use in the Roman Army as short swords (Bishop 2016a: 28), reflecting the external pressures on fashion within the Roman Empire and, possibly, paving the way for evolution in *spatha* forms. Indeed, some 2nd/3rd-century AD *spathae* were given riveted ring pommels, possibly when a tang broke and needed repairing.

LATER PRINCIPATE

A large number of *spathae* have been recovered from the various waterlogged sites of Thorsberg (Germany) and Ejsbøl, Illerup Ådal, Nydam and Vimose (Denmark). Although there are earlier and later weapons, the bulk of the swords from these sites date to the 2nd and 3rd centuries AD. It is apparent that the swords from these sites not only included Roman weapons, but also Roman-influenced swords, and in some cases (particularly noticeable among the scabbard fittings) Roman equipment customized in the local traditions. These large assemblages skew our data on *spathae* but also provide invaluable information on the swords, which is why they are so important.

The 2nd century AD saw the introduction of two new forms (and countless variants) of the *spatha*: the Lauriacum/Hromówka and the Straubing/Nydam types. To all intents and purposes these were two different swords with a common ancestry and their persistence into the 4th century AD (albeit with differing classifications) only serves to confirm this.

The Lauriacum/Hromówka type of blade (Miks 2007: 92–98) is named after examples from the civil settlement outside the legionary fortress of Lorch-Lauriacum (Austria) and from a tumulus near Hromówka (Ukraine), the latter example folded back on itself three times (ritually 'killed'). The blade was broad (usually in the range of 50mm to 67mm) and normally featured a triangular point. In many ways, its form is reminiscent of the earlier (and smaller) Pompeii-type *gladius*. Lengths varied between 580mm and 795mm. In terms of the proportions of the blade, it was usually in the region of 1:10. Miks has identified a number of variants to this basic category, including the Mainz/Canterbury, Hromówka and Straubing/Hromówka.

From a dating point of view, one of the most important later Principate Lauriacum/Hromówka *spathae* to have been excavated comes from a burial at Lyon-Lugdunum (France). Found with a dozen silver coins, the latest of which was a *denarius* of AD 194, its most likely context is the battle fought at Lugdunum by Septimius Severus against the former commander of the Roman Army in Britain, now usurper, Clodius Albinus in AD 197 (Wuilleumier 1950). The *spatha* may well have belonged to one of the British legionaries who fought on the losing side. It was broken in two and lacked its tip, but the blade survived to 684mm in length, and part of the tang and a copper-alloy hand guard plate were present. It was recovered along with components from its scabbard, baldric fittings, and a waist belt formed from copper-alloy letters spelling out the motto FELIX VTERE ('use and be lucky').

An intriguing burial found in Canterbury (Kent, England), also dating to the late 2nd century AD, contained two Roman soldiers, interred one above the other, and both equipped with Lauriacum/Hromówka *spathae* with double parallel fullers. The swords were far from identical, however. The lower sword was the larger, had a slightly tapering, lenticular-sectioned blade and no discernible transition to its point, and was evidently in a sheath with a copper-alloy peltate chape with volutes. The upper sword had a flat-sectioned, parallel-edged blade and distinct, triangular point, found with a simple, copper-alloy peltate chape. Weapons burials were extremely unusual in the Roman Army at this date and the circumstances of the burial (it was illegal to bury within a town), together with the date and the location, may be reason also to connect these swords with the civil war between Severus and Albinus. Above all, it is interesting that two such diverse swords could be found in service together.

The Straubing/Nydam type of *spatha* (Miks 2007: 80–92) is named after an example from a *villa rustica* – an establishment principally intended to supply the Roman Army on the nearby frontier – at Straubing in southern Germany, while several examples of the Nydam weapon came from a votive deposit in water in what is now Denmark. The form is characterized by a slender blade (usually falling between 34mm and 49mm) with a rounded tip. Lengths varied between 590mm and 777mm. The proportions of this form of blade were usually in the

Blade cross-sections. (Drawings M.C. Bishop)

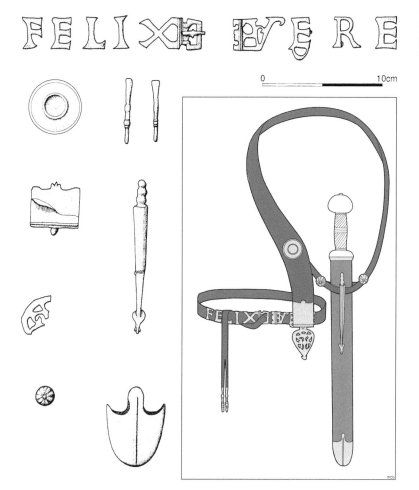

The *spatha*, baldric and belt fittings from the Lyon burial (France). (Drawings & reconstruction M.C. Bishop)

region of 1:16. Miks identified Newstead, Nydam, Straubing, Eining and Ejsbøl variants of this type.

A complete Straubing/Nydam *spatha* and scabbard were found at Hoege Werd near De Meern, Utrecht (Netherlands) in a watery context (Aarts 2012: 235). The lenticular-sectioned blade tapered and displayed a degree of distal taper, but there were no fullers. The tripartite handle assembly was made from lime wood. The pommel was spherical and held in place by the tang being peened over a circular washer. The hand grip was oval in cross-section with three ridges forming four indentations for the fingers. The hand guard was of the near-spherical type. The iron scabbard slide and simple, peltate chape served to date the find to the later 2nd or early 3rd century AD. Other Straubing/Nydam-type *spathae* in the Netherlands are known from Alem, Empel, Lobith and Rossum, all similarly from watery deposits.

A river find of another Straubing/Nydam-type sword was made at Bodenham (Herefordshire, England) in 2003. A date in the late 2nd or early 3rd century AD is suggested by its lenticular cross-section, but there was unfortunately no clear archaeological context evidence to support this. There were no fullers and the sword was bent along the whole length of its blade.

A sword from a burial at Khisfine, in the Golan (Syria), is remarkable for the scabbard found with it. Probably a Straubing/Nydam-type *spatha*, although it lacks some of its blade, it had ivory hilt components, a theme which was continued in its unusual scabbard (see page 50). The dimensions of its scabbard suggest that the sword may originally have been up to 600mm long (Gogräfe & Chehadé 1999: 74).

During the Sassanid Persian siege of Dura-Europos (also in Syria), usually dated to AD 256, the attackers attempted to drive a mine under Tower 19 on the west wall of the town. The Roman defenders intercepted it with a countermine and a fierce battle took place underground, during which some of the Romans lost their swords. One of these Lauriacum/Hromówka-type swords survived complete, albeit now in six conjoining pieces. Lenticular in cross-section, there was no trace of a fuller on the blade. On the tang, however, mineralized traces of the wooden pommel, grip and hand guard were visible, the grain of the grip running along the tang and that of the pommel and guard across it. The similarly preserved remains of a scabbard still adhered to the surface of the blade, revealing that it was formed from two thin wooden sheets apparently wrapped in textile (James 2004: 145–47).

Another complete (but now fragmentary) Lauriacum/Hromówka-type sword was found in a hypocaust within the city at Dura-Europos along with its bone chape and traces of a wooden scabbard. The sword, which lacks the tip of its tang, has a lenticular-sectioned blade which appears to have fullers, although this may be the result of differential corrosion on a pattern-welded weapon (James 2004: 145).

Neither of these swords from Dura-Europos have scabbard slides associated with them so these may have been made of wood, just as that of the Khisfine sword was made of the same material as its scabbard. The weapon from Khisfine had a damaged (Straubing/Nydam?) blade, so its full length is unknown. However, this sword is best known for its handle and scabbard, because both were made of ivory. In fact, the pommel, handle and hand guard had all evidently been carved from one tusk. The sheath was formed from two pieces of ivory (in much the same way that wooden sheaths were formed from two sheets of wood), with an integral disc chape at the bottom and a scabbard runner on the front face.

There are also *spathae* from the German *limes* dating from the time of the abandonment of that frontier in the middle of the 3rd century AD. These include notable examples from Rainau-Buch and Straubing. The Rainau-Buch blade was included in a hoard (which included arrows, javelin heads and catapult bolts) from the abandonment deposit of a Roman frontier fort dating from that period. Unsurprisingly, the blade from Straubing is the type-find for the Straubing/Nydam type of *spatha*, although the largest number of these come from outside the Roman Empire from the northern votive sites, including Nydam.

A Straubing/Nydam-type sword was recovered from a cremation burial at Grabice in Poland, along with an inlaid circular box chape, a spear, axe, spurs and brooches. The blade of the sword bore a Roman maker's stamp (NATALIS M) and incorporated two parallel fullers. The

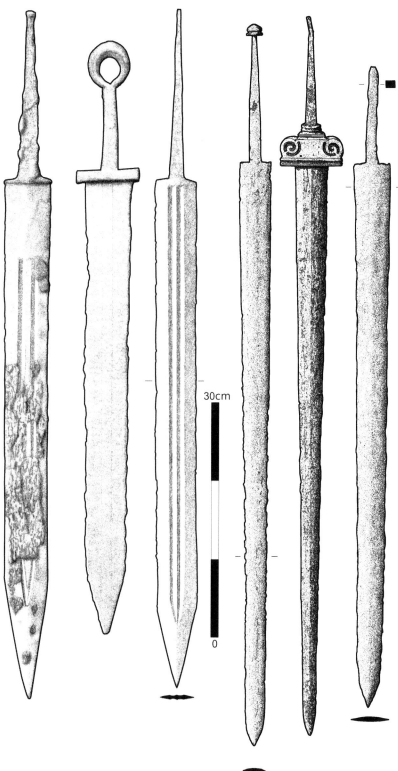

30cm

0

17

whole weapon was folded in three, perhaps as a ritual 'killing' of it, and can be dated to the middle of the 3rd century AD.

Finally, a handle assembly from Dorchester (Dorset, England), consisting of a hand guard, grip and pommel of bone, probably belongs to this period, rather than to an earlier *gladius* or *spatha*, or later *spatha*. The hand grip lacks the characteristic faceting of early Principate *gladii* and finds of military equipment in Romano-British towns of the 2nd and 3rd centuries AD are by no means rare.

The Lauriacum/Hromówka and Straubing/Nydam types were the principal forms of *spatha* for more than a century, once the long sword became the main weapon of both Roman infantry and cavalry. However, there is no clear evidence of any differentiation in blade type between legionary and auxiliary troops, or between infantry and cavalry.

One of the consequences of the displacement of the short *gladius* by the longer *spatha* was, all too obviously, the absence of a short sword for infantry who needed or liked it. This was resolved (possibly on an ad hoc basis) by the introduction of the *semispatha*, often made from cut-down broken *spathae* (Bishop 2016a: 28–32). In some swords – those from Köngen (Germany) and Künzing (Germany) for instance – where fullers ran right to the sword tip, the truncation of the original blade (both originally of the Lauriacum/Hromówka type, probably) is very obvious. This suggests there were issues with swords breaking in use, perhaps because they had begun to be used in a manner for which they were never intended (blade-on-blade fencing), although this is pure speculation.

Two views of a silver-inlaid circular box chape from the 3rd century AD. (Photo © P. Gross/Arachne)

DOMINATE

The narrow Straubing/Nydam type of *spatha* was succeeded by the Illerup/Wyhl type (Miks 2007: 99–103), finds of which date from the

middle of the 3rd century AD onwards. The later form of the Straubing/ Nydam type, termed the Ejsbøl variant by Miks, was primarily dated to the 4th century AD. Most finds, as the variant name suggests, came from the 'bog' find at Ejsbøl (Denmark). There was a considerable variety in dimensions, but blades were usually between 42mm and 57.5mm in width. Lengths fell between 650mm and 830mm. Illerup/Wyhl *spathae*, by comparison, were between 620mm and 852mm in length and 42mm and 57mm in width. A fine example of a Late Roman Illerup/Wyhl *spatha* came from a grave under the church of St Severin in Köln (Germany) which included a circular silver scabbard 'box' chape inlaid with niello and a complete handle assembly of hand guard, hand grip, pommel and peen block.

The Osterburken/Kemathen type of *spatha* (Miks 2007: 104–05), on the other hand, seems to have been even later, stretching from the 4th into the 5th centuries AD and continuing the tradition of the Lauriacum/ Hromówka type. Blades ranging between 60mm and 77mm in width and between 715mm and 885mm in length are known. The Osterburken (Germany) example, with a single, broad fuller, came from a post-Roman deposit in the ditch of the long-abandoned frontier fort. That from Kemathen (Germany) was found in a 5th-century AD burial.

A few examples of what has been classed as the Asiatic type of *spatha* (Miks 2007: 106) come from 5th-century AD burials across Western Europe, such as one from Dijon (France). With their metal hand guards

Asiatic-type *spatha* from Katzelsdorf (A341; Austria). (Photo N. Weigl, © Landessammlungen Niederösterreich)

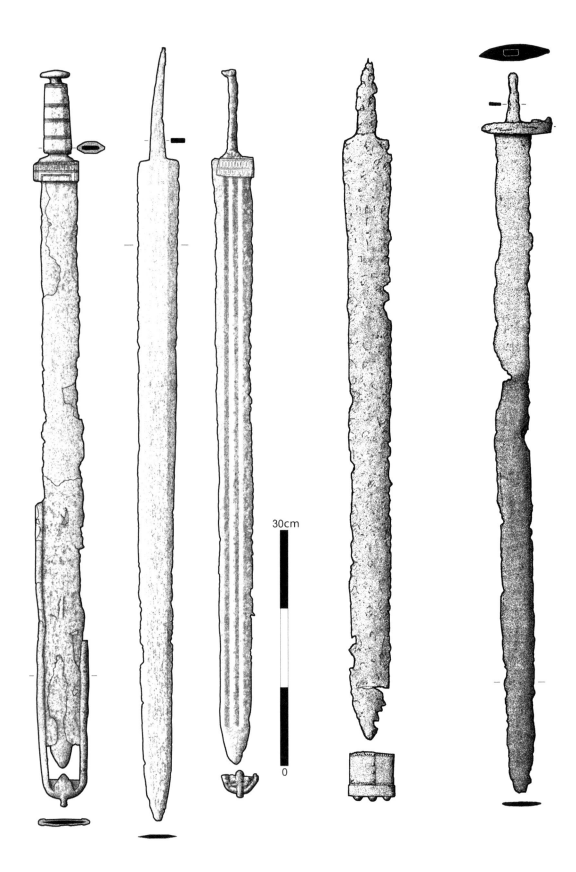

30cm

0

(in effect prototype medieval quillons), these weapons are reminiscent of both ring-pommel swords of an earlier time and later Germanic swords.

Late Roman *spathae* (almost invariably sheathed) feature in a number of representational sources. Although the swords depicted on the Four Tetrarchs in St Mark's Basilica in Venice (Italy) have eagle-headed pommels, like the swords of earlier emperors, they also have Gundremmingen-type chapes on the scabbards, as well as waisted scabbard runners (but no baldrics), indicating that they were in fact supposed to represent *spathae*.

OPPOSITE LEFT
Illerup/Wyhl swords from Hemmingen (A293, Germany), Ejsbøl (A146,21, Denmark) and Abingdon (A2, Oxfordshire, England). (Drawings M.C. Bishop)

OPPOSITE RIGHT
An Osterburken/Kemathen-type *spatha* with a Gundremmingen-type chape from Zalaszengrót (A809; Hungary) and an Asiatic-type *spatha* from Vienna (A780; Austria). (Drawings M.C. Bishop)

21

SPATHA SIZES	TOTAL LENGTH (mm)	BLADE LENGTH (mm)	BLADE WIDTH (mm)	TIP LENGTH (mm)	THICKNESS (mm)	MUSEUM
Early Principate						
Unprovenanced	820	745	39	–	?	Private collection
Newstead 1 (A526)	774	622	35	*c.*84	?	National Museums of Scotland (Edinburgh)
Newstead 2 (A527)	*c.*773	635	35	*c.*64	?	National Museums of Scotland (Edinburgh)
Falkirk (A94)	835	677	*c.*45	>58	*c.*6	Falkirk Museum
Rottweil (A617)	770	650	38	*c.*48	*c.*4.5	Dominikanermuseum (Rottweil)
Diersheim (A125)	785	627	38	*c.*52	?	Badisches Landesmuseum (Karlsruhe)
Iža (A326)	885	735	47	*c.*58	?	Roman and Ethnographic Museum Kelemantia (Iža)
Later Principate						
Lyon (A454)	754	>684	52	?	?	Musée de Fourvière (Lyon)
Canterbury 1 (A95,1)	870	655	59	*c.*149	?	Canterbury Roman Museum
Canterbury 2 (A95,2)	915	690	56	*c.*64	?	Canterbury Roman Museum
Khisfine (A349)	520	>520	40	?	?	Syrian National Museum (Damascus)
Dura-Europos (A140)	855	695	60	*c.*40	?	Yale University Art Gallery (New Haven)
Dura-Europos (A139)	790	645	50–59	*c.*44	?	Syrian National Museum (Damascus)
De Meern	740	540	45	*c.*50	4.5–3.5	Castellum Hoge Woerd (Utrecht)
Bodenham	775	660	38	*c.*70	*c.*6	Herefordshire Museums (Hereford)
Straubing (A700)	940	797	46	*c.*25	?	Gäubodenmuseum (Straubing)
Nydam (A536,1)	881	758	40.5	*c.*38	*c.*8	Nationalmuseet (Copenhagen)
Lorch (A447)	810	655	65	*c.*84	?	Oberösterreichisches Landesmuseum (Linz)
Hromówka (A311)	778	648	64	*c.*80	*c.*5	Muzeum Archeologiczne (Kraków)
Köngen (A359)	392	312	60	*c.*46	*c.*6	Landesmuseum Württemberg (Stuttgart)
Künzing (A399)	494	337	*c.*56	*c.*36	*c.*6	Archäologische Staatssammlung (Munich)
Dominate						
Köln (A357)	905	730	41	*c.*88	*c.*5	Rheinisches Landesmuseum (Bonn)
Illerup Ådal (A321,41)	905	790	42	*c.*44	*c.*6	Moesgaard Museum (Højbjerg)
Ejsbøl (A146,29)	912	792	*c.*51	*c.*80	*c.*5	Museum Sønderjylland (Haderslev)
Wyhl (A798)	900	*c.*780	*c.*52	*c.*56	*c.*4	Landesamt für Denkmalpflege Baden-Württemberg
Osterburken (A561,1)	920	815	60	*c.*44	*c.*6	Badisches Landesmuseum (Karlsruhe)
Kemathen (A342)	900	*c.*785	*c.*77	*c.*60	*c.*8	Archäologische Staatssammlung (Munich)
Dijon (A126,2)	915	792	*c.*50	*c.*52	*c.*8	Musée Archéologique (Dijon)

NB: Thicknesses have been estimated from published cross-sections at one-quarter scale, so are only approximations.

MANUFACTURE

Early long swords of the type brought into the Roman Army by auxiliary cavalry under the late Republic and in the early years of the Roman Empire were long thought not to be of the highest quality. This was doubtless due to Polybius' comment (*Histories* 2.33.6) that Celtic swords lacked a point and were good for only one blow before bending. Metallographic analysis of a selection of La Tène swords shows this was not necessarily the case, however (Pleiner 1993: 142–43, 147). In fact, a wide variety of types of manufacture have been noted, although that need not mean Polybius was wrong, merely that he may have witnessed this himself once and was generalizing from the particular.

During the 1st century AD, blade manufacture for the *spatha* seems to have been indistinguishable from that of the *gladius*, with steel edges normally welded onto an iron core. This is scarcely surprising, given that the former was essentially an extended version of the latter. There were variations, however. A *spatha* from Augst in Switzerland (Miks A24,1) was examined scientifically and revealed to have been

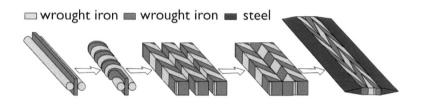

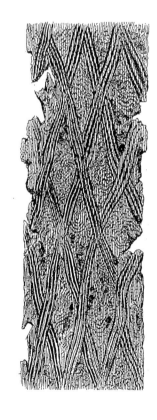
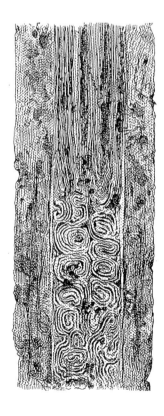

These drawings, after Birch 2013 and incorporating engravings from Engelhardt 1869, depict pattern-welded swords and show the idealized process (above) and the results (below). (Drawings M.C. Bishop)

23

produced by fire-welding a layer of steel between two layers of iron, providing it with steel edges (Williams 2012: 55). The newer forms of blade introduced in the 2nd century AD, however, also saw more innovative manufacturing techniques. Principal among these was the use of what is commonly known as pattern welding, whereby strips of steel were entwined during the forging process to form the core, but which could also be used as a decorative component, perhaps enhanced by etching. Sword blades could also be adorned with metal inlay, a purely decorative component with no function. While it is uncertain, however, whether pattern welding strengthened a blade or was purely decorative (Birch 2013), inlay was certainly purely decorative and could even potentially weaken the sword blade, partly as a result of the potential for bimetallic electrolytic corrosion if the blade was not kept clean.

Sword blades could also be made lighter by means of fullers (sometimes, incorrectly, referred to as 'blood channels'). These were effectively forged, longitudinal corrugations that reduced the amount of metal used while not compromising the strength of a blade. They were not used on Republican or early Principate *gladii* or *spathae*, although they do feature on pre-Roman Iberian short swords, as well as some Roman daggers. A range of types of fuller were in use for later Principate *spathae*, usually as two narrow V-sectioned or one broad U-sectioned, channels and they could be one- (asymmetric) or two-sided (symmetric). It is by no means clear, however, to what extent these were aesthetic, as opposed to

Anatomy of a *spatha* (opposite)

This plate depicts the three main types of *spatha* with examples of their respective scabbards. The Pompeii-type sword (**1**) has a decorated scabbard adorned with embossed brass plates, which were tinned to produce a pleasing visual contrast. With a pronounced point and parallel-edged blade, it is suitable for both cutting and thrusting. The Lauriacum/ Hromówka blade (**2**) was comparatively short and broad, with a triangular point, and could be used for stabbing, while the Straubing/Nydam-type sword (**3**), with a longer, narrower tapering blade, could be used for chopping.

The 'business-end' of the *spatha* was the point or *mucro*. Rounded on the Straubing/Nydam and Illerup/Wyhl types, more pointed on the Pompeii and Lauriacum/Hromówka types, it fulfilled the first of the important functions of the sword: stabbing (*punctim*), although the latter two types were clearly better suited for this. Next came the blade (*lamina*) with two cutting edges (*acies*) which provided the second function of the sword: chopping or cutting (*caesim*). Both the tip and blade generally had a diamond-shaped, or occasionally lenticular,

cross-section, but the Straubing/Nydam and Lauriacum/ Hromówka types could incorporate fullers (*alvei*) and inlaid decoration near the hilt. The narrow, rectangular-sectioned tang (*cauda*) held the various elements of the hilt (*capulus*), consisting of the hand guard and its basal brass hand guard plate; the hand grip; the pommel; and the peen block. As with the *gladius*, the peen block may itself have been used as a secondary weapon in a similar manner to the 'skull-crusher' on the Fairbairn-Sykes commando knife.

The scabbard (*vagina*) for the Pompeii type consisted of a mouth plate at the top and a terminal knob at the bottom with the sides made of U-sectioned copper-alloy binding (or guttering). Metal plates could be added for decoration, including the locket plate at the top and the chape at the bottom. Suspension bands were normally riveted to the guttering and held freely moving suspension rings. Scabbards for both the Straubing/Nydam and Lauriacum/Hromówka types were less ornate, with scabbard runners for suspension and peltate, box, or circular chapes to protect the tip of the blade.

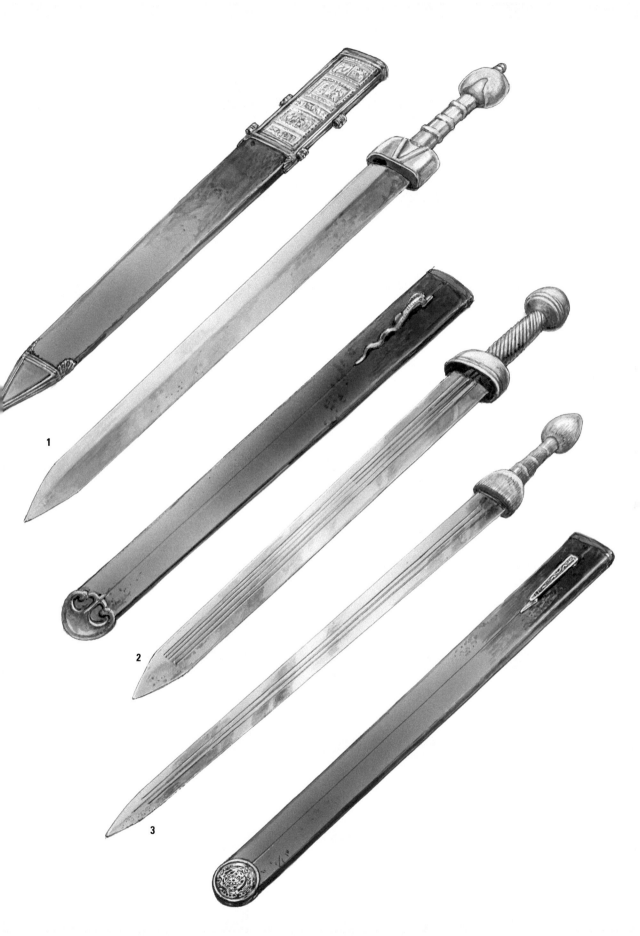

1

2

3

practical, variations. Earlier Principate cross-sections tended to be lenticular, but faceted (normally hexagonal) cross-sections appear on later Principate blades on both Straubing/Nydam and Lauriacum/Hromówka types when they do not employ fullers. A letter from Theodoric, king of Italy, written in the 6th century AD and describing some swords sent as a gift, uses the term *alveus* ('groove' or 'channel') for a fuller (Davidson 1962: 106).

Pattern welding appeared on a large scale at the same time as the new *spathae* were introduced into the Roman Army in the 2nd century AD. The basic principle of pattern welding involved fire-welding several rods (usually four or more) together and imparting a twist in the process. This then formed the core of the blade and steel edges were fire-welded on either side. Although a new technique for Roman smiths, something resembling it had been around among Celtic smiths since at least the 3rd century BC, as was demonstrated by Pleiner (1993: 167). Moreover, analysis has even shown it in use on an Etruscan blade from the 7th century BC (Nicodemi *et al.* 2005).

Besides pattern welding, blades could be inlaid or 'damascened', which has sometimes been confused with the notion of 'Damascus steel'. The Romans were already skilled at damascening dagger scabbards in the 1st century AD, however, before they did it on *spatha* blades (see page 49).

In the 1st century AD, the bulk of equipment manufacture seems to have been undertaken by the Roman Army itself. The evidence suggests, however, that from the 2nd century AD onwards sword production was evidently in the hands of both the Army and private craftsmen (presumably Army veterans who used their retirement to continue their trade). A papyrus from Egypt recording work undertaken in a legionary workshop (*ChLA* 409), probably at Nicopolis (in modern-day Greece), includes an entry for 17 April of an unknown year (but possibly in the

2nd century AD) for '] *spathar[u]m fabricatae X*' or '10 swords made'. It notes that there were legionaries and auxiliaries, as well as civilians, working in the *fabrica* that day. When those soldiers retired from service, some at least may well have become craftsmen in the private arms trade.

One clear sign of private production is thought to be makers' stamps on sword blades. Something like 6 per cent of Roman sword blades bear such stamps, the majority being *spathae* from the northern votive deposits from Vimose, Nydam and Illerup Ådal, although a few examples are known from within the bounds of the Roman Empire. These stamps often take the form of symbols such as rosettes, half-moons and quadrants – possibly quality assurance marks – but others include Latin inscriptions naming the producer, such as COGILLVS, NATALIS and DORICCVS. It is likely that the stamps were applied when the blade was hot, rather than cold-stamped.

By the Late Roman period, Army manufacture had been formalized into state *fabricae*, each specializing in particular products. One of the stamps from Illerup Ådal reads FDNAVG which has been interpreted as an abbreviation for *F(abrica) D(omini) N(ostri) Aug(usti)* ('workshop of Our Lord the Emperor'). The *Notitia Dignitatum* lists *fabricae spathariae* at Lucca-Luca (Italy) and Reims-Remi (France), but it is possible that the many sites listed as *scutaris et armorum* ('shields and weaponry') were also producing swords. The *Price Edict* issued by Diocletian in AD 301 mentions both *spathae* (the maximum cost allowed for sharpening a sword was 25 *denarii*) and their scabbards (maximum cost for manufacture 100 *denarii*), however, so was presumably reflecting a continued private trade in weaponry into the Late Roman period.

Lauriacum/Hromówka sword from the River Kupa near Sisak-Siscia (Croatia) with a detail of the inlaid brass figure of a warrior near the tang. (Photos Filip Beusan, © Archaeological Museum Zagreb)

USE
The cut and thrust

INTERPRETING THE EVIDENCE

The deposition of booty into water was widely practised in antiquity and is typified by one tribe of Gauls: 'Upon returning to their old settlements near Toulouse, the Tectosagi were struck by a plague and did not recover from it, until, being warned by admonitions from their soothsayers, they threw the gold and silver they had acquired in war and sacrilege into the lake of Toulouse' (Justinus, *Epitome* 32.3.8–90). The main reason we know so much about the *spatha* during the later Principate and Dominate periods is the value of the weapon to Rome's neighbours. Finds of Roman weaponry from Northern European votive deposits around water, often referred to (rather inaccurately, because most were open water at the time of deposition) as 'bog' finds, far outweigh any other archaeological source (Rald 1994). Both Roman and Roman-influenced swords come from a number of such sites, as well as from funerary contexts within the Przeworsk Culture in what is now Poland, and reveal just how substantial the movement of weaponry from the Roman Empire to Barbaricum – the world beyond the empire – was between AD 150 and 450. What remains unclear (and the source of much discussion among scholars) is whether this resulted from trade, booty or a combination of factors including service in the Roman Army by Germanic troops from beyond the imperial frontiers.

THE CAVALRY *SPATHA* TO AD 100

The use of non-Roman cavalry during the Republican period, notably by Julius Caesar in Gaul and by Crassus in Syria, inevitably saw the introduction of new weapons into Roman field armies, particularly the long sword of the 'Celtic' auxiliary cavalry. Despite what seems to be a general contempt in the literary sources for long, poor-quality swords being waved around, what we now recognize as *spatha*-like weapons were to become important for cavalry once the long *gladius Hispaniensis* fell from favour and was replaced by shorter blades for infantry use.

The debate about how the sword should be used (to stab or cut) – evidently ongoing with the *gladius* while it was in service – was to some extent irrelevant while the *spatha* was a purely cavalry weapon, because a cutting motion was the most natural on horseback and was indeed derived from its ancestry. The manner in which it was wielded might feel alien to the modern swordsman, because only a limited amount of flexion in the wrist was possible, given the size of most hand guards. This just meant that more leverage was put into the blow from the downward movement of the arm and it would be no particular hardship for a man trained to fight that way.

The use of the sword in this period was invariably linked to the way in which Roman auxiliary cavalry were used on the battlefield. As the name of their units (*alae* – literally 'wings') implies, they were deployed on the wings of the main infantry formation and generally only called upon once the enemy had broken and was in retreat. This was when they would chase down their fleeing foes and cut them down as they ran, either with javelins, a thrusting spear, or with the long sword. The cavalry of the mixed units, the *cohortes equitatae*, seem to have been brigaded with the *alae* during major set-piece battles, if Arrian (in his *Ektaxis kata Alanon*) is to be believed. As they were used in the same way as their higher-status brethren, it seems likely that they too were equipped with the *spatha*. The infantry in those units, however, like those in the legions and the auxiliary infantry cohorts, were armed with the shorter *gladius*,

The battle for Gelduba c.69 AD (overleaf)

Auxiliary cavalry loyal to the Roman force under Dillius Vocula join battle with Batavian rebels, having sallied out from the gateway of a temporary camp at Gelduba (modern-day Krefeld-Gellep in Germany) on the west bank of the Rhine. They are equipped almost identically and can only really be distinguished by shield colour and design (the Batavians may have chosen to paint over the Roman blazons on theirs). Fortunately, the Roman *ala* here has oval shields and the Batavian cavalry hexagonal ones, but it cannot always have been that easy to distinguish friend from foe. Both sides are using the Pompeii-type *spatha* to hack at opposing riders and their horses – large numbers of dead horses have been excavated where they fell on the site – but the occasional thrust with the tip of the weapon is used at the face of an opponent. The conflict is evenly matched, as both sides are similarly equipped and equally well practised at this sort of encounter. Parrying with the shield while holding the reins is difficult, but is assisted by the close bond between the rider and his horse and the firm and secure seat provided by the four-horned Roman saddle. Although most of the combat tends to be on the shielded side, some men are recklessly fighting from their unshielded sides, so desperate is the situation.

CROMANIVS

Sheathed *spatha* on the cavalry tombstone of Romanius Capito from Mainz (Germany) using a shafted weapon.
(Photo: akg-images/Interfoto/Toni Schneiders)

examples of both types of sword being found together in the *cohors equitata* fort at Vindolanda near Hadrian's Wall.

This employment of cavalry for 'mopping up' helps to explain why casualty figures in battles between Romans and barbarians were usually so disproportionately high: most deaths occurred once an enemy turned to flee. Cavalry could also be employed for scouting or skirmishing (something Arrian also describes), but in any of these roles the advantages of a blade with a long reach would have been obvious.

Every legion contained a small contingent of 120 horsemen (*equites legionum*) who seem mainly to have been employed for communication purposes. It has been suggested that they were not only organized as part of the infantry formation but were actually drawn from legionaries who could ride. Even so, they could be used in combat, as Tacitus (*Annals* 4.73.2; *Histories* 1.57) attests. While none of our sources state unequivocally how they were armed, the tombstone of Tiberius Claudius Maximus, a legionary cavalryman with *legio VII Claudia* credited with killing the Dacian king Decebalus, seems on the one hand to imply that he was equipped with two spears or javelins and a sword, although whether this was indeed the *spatha* is not clear from the relief. On the other hand, the *eques legionis* Caius Marius from Bonn is not shown with a sword, just a thrusting spear.

Thus the evidence points to use of the *spatha* being confined to the auxiliary cavalry of the *alae* and *cohortes equitae* during the latter part of the 1st century BC and the whole of the 1st century AD. In the 2nd century AD, however, there was an important change.

THE *SPATHA* IN THE LATER PRINCIPATE

It is difficult to identify precisely when it happened, but the use of the long sword began to spread beyond just the auxiliary cavalry. No surviving source records the reason for switching from the short to the long sword for infantry, however. Although it is tempting to ascribe such a change to 'military reforms', this is probably unwise: the *Historia Augusta* famously recorded that Hadrian 'reformed the equipment' of the troops in Germany while there, but what this meant in practice – and indeed whether it even happened in quite such a neat way as the text implies – is far from clear. The Roman Empire and its army were not structured in such a way that global reforms could easily be instituted. With communication between Rome and its frontiers often taking weeks or even months, change was inevitably going to be gradual. In fact, some sort of imperial decree is far less likely than a process taking months or even years, perhaps communicated among units when they met on campaigns such as the suppression of the Bar Kochba revolt under Hadrian, the Armenian and Parthian Wars of Lucius Verus or Marcus Aurelius' Marcomannic Wars. Legions from different provinces met up for such major conflicts and that would provide at least one way in which developments could be communicated and ideas exchanged. For this reason, it is far harder to pinpoint when and where the change from *gladius* to *spatha* started than it would be if an emperor had ordered it at a particular time and in a particular place.

Is it possible to see this process in operation among the archaeological evidence? Swords themselves are comparatively rare finds within the bounds of the Roman Empire, but the fittings associated with their scabbards are much more common and may indeed enable us to

RIGHT
Lauriacum/Hromówka-type
spatha from Medinet Habu
(Egypt). (Photo © Royal
Ontario Museum)

FAR RIGHT
Lauriacum/Hromówka-type
spatha and scabbard
reconstructed by Robert
Wimmers. (Photo © R. Wimmers)

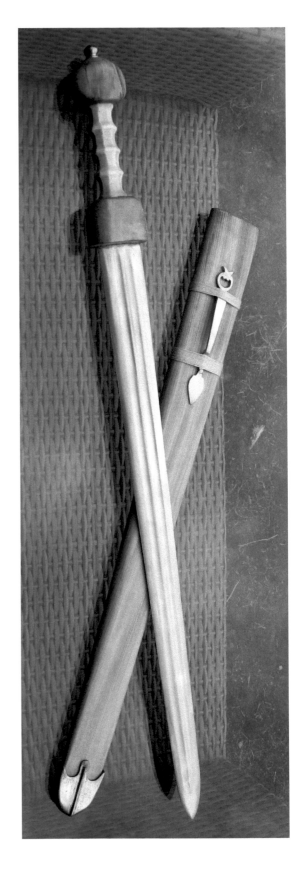

understand the process. A useful benchmark for the adoption of the *spatha* is provided by the burial from near Lyon which included a Lauriacum/Hromówka-type *spatha* and its scabbard (see page 15). As the coin evidence from the grave suggests that this dated to the battle of Lugdunum in AD 197, it provides a convenient *terminus ante quem*. The abandonment of sites just after the middle of the 2nd century AD, notably forts on and around the Antonine Wall in Scotland and those involved in the Marcomannic Wars on the Danube in Germany, produce similar fittings to those from the Lyon burial, so the process seems already to have been under way by the middle of that century. At the same time, archaeological layers on sites producing military equipment that can be dated to the Hadrianic period do not include the sort of fittings associated with the infantry adoption of the *spatha*. Thus the middle of the 2nd century AD seems to be the key period for the initiation of this change – but why did it happen?

Linked to the widespread adoption of the *spatha* was the change in the means of carriage. The classic sword belt or baldric attached to

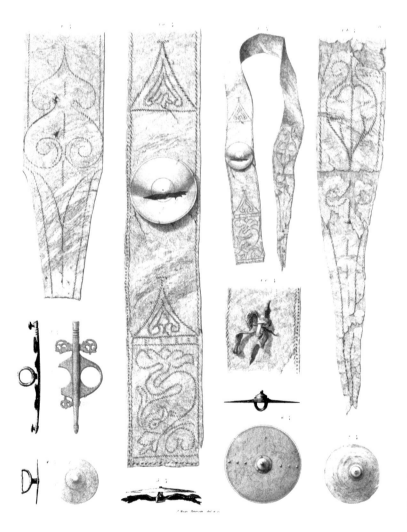

This illustration from Engelhardt 1869 depicts a leather baldric of the 2nd/3rd century AD from Vimose (Denmark). (Author)

35

suspension rings on either side of the scabbard on the right hip gave way to a broader baldric passing through a slide or runner fixed to the front of the scabbard, which was now worn on the left hip. At the end of the 1st and beginning of the 2nd centuries AD, some legionaries (depicted on a column base from Mainz in Germany) and auxiliaries (shown on metopes from the Tropaeum Traiani at Adamclisi in Romania) were already using scabbards on the left hip, so the change to the long blade and its new means of carriage were not necessarily connected. This style of suspension – because it broke with a long tradition – is symptomatic of a substantial cultural change within the Roman Army. Sculptural evidence also indicates that the sword scabbard not only changed sides but was also worn appreciably lower than was the case with the *gladius* or the earlier cavalry *spatha*. Both of these weapons are typically shown with the pommel as high as the armpit, whereas the later *spatha* has it slightly lower.

The major change this would have imposed would have been the way in which the sword was drawn. Worn on the right-hand side, the sword would be gripped thumb downwards and drawn vertically upwards until clear of the scabbard (although a degree of angling became possible, the further it was withdrawn). When on the left-hand side, it would be drawn across the body, behind the shield. Although the action of drawing a sword suspended on the right-hand side could be carried through directly into a cutting blow by the skilled practitioner, a sword drawn across the body from the left would always need an extra movement to strike. It might also require a little more elbow-room: 'Presently our infantry was also left unsupported, while the different units became so crammed together that a soldier could hardly draw his sword, or withdraw his hand after he had reached out' (Ammianus, *Res Gestae* 31.13.2). In other words, the change had to have been worth it.

That is still not an adequate explanation for why the change to the *spatha* happened, however. There must have been something about the attributes of the longer sword that made it more appealing than the shorter *gladius*. As the *spatha* of the early 2nd century AD was essentially an elongated version of the Pompeii-type *gladius* in its form (see page 10), part of the answer may have been the additional reach provided by the blade that was central to its adoption. However, the conflicting views as to the best type of blow with the *gladius* that we see in the sources (Bishop 2016a: 64–65) – to stab (*punctim*) or to cut (*caesim*) – may mean that the short Pompeii-type *gladius* was deemed inadequate for the sort of dual-purpose use that the old *gladius Hispaniensis* was capable of. Does this then imply a change in the style of hand-to-hand combat among Roman infantry? It may certainly reflect the fact that the manner of infantry combat had been gradually evolving, but it is unlikely that there was a sudden change demanding different weapons. Rather it indicates conservatism within the way the Roman Army fought hand-to-hand and that the *spatha* was seen as the perfect compromise between stabbing and cutting blows while providing additional reach.

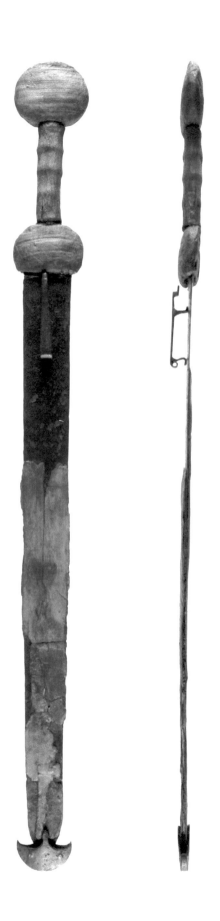

Straubing/Nydam sword from
De Meern, Utrecht (Netherlands).
(Photos © Restaura)

When the Late Roman author Vegetius came to write about the weaponry of his *antiqua legio*, the 'old legion' he (or, at least, his source) was describing had already changed from short to long swords: 'They were heavily armed, because they had helmets, cuirasses, greaves, shields, large swords (which they call *spathae*) and other small ones (which they name *semispathae*), and five *plumbatae* placed in a shield, which they throw during the first assault' (Vegetius, *DRM* 2.15). The place of *semispathae* – often but not always cut-down *spathae* – as the short swords of the later Principate period may be explicable in a reluctance to give up the shorter weapon on the part of some members of the military (Bishop 2016a: 28–32) which could be termed the 'conservatism' scenario. It might equally be interpreted as a sign of desperation in the face of continuous warfare, poor-quality swordsmithing, and a shortage of the sort of resources and skills necessary to make long swords at a sufficient rate (what might be termed the 'decline' scenario). There may even have been other factors at play, but the available information is insufficient for a firm conclusion to be reached, other than to note that short swords were indeed still used in the 3rd century AD and that they were often made out of damaged long swords.

One other issue that needs to be addressed is the clear division of these newer *spathae* into two principal types. There is always the possibility that there was functional difference, reflecting use by different types of troops. Could, for example, Lauriacum/Hromówka-type *spathae* have been used by legionary infantry and Straubing/Nydam-type *spathae* by auxiliaries, or even just cavalry? One way to test such a hypothesis might be by plotting the find spots of all of the known swords found on Roman military sites. Although initially attractive (Lorch-Lauriacum was a legionary base and Straubing-Sorviodunum a part-mounted unit fort), the results are far from conclusive.

DOMINATE

By the time of the Tetrarchy at the end of the 3rd century AD, the *spatha*, now worn on the left hip, was firmly established as the sword of the Late Roman period. *Semispathae* appear to have fallen from favour, perhaps as a result of the increasingly Germanic nature of much of the Roman Army. This process, often termed 'barbarization' by scholars in the past, was far more subtle than that term implies – indeed, it can plausibly be argued that the Roman Army was 'barbarizing' from the Republican period onwards! – and doubtless was as much a fashion trend as it was a reflection of its ethnic composition.

So it was that the famous purple porphyry group now built into the exterior of St Mark's Basilica in Venice sees the four embracing tetrarchs

Imperial statue from Alba Iulia (Romania) depicting the 3rd-century AD military 'identity': ring-buckle waist belt (with fastening studs) and a *spatha* in its scabbard (with a circular chape) suspended from a broad baldric. (Photo © J.C.N. Coulston)

Standard-bearer from Chesters fort (Northumberland, England) wearing his sword on his left hip and dagger on the right. (Photo © M.C. Bishop)

equipped with *spathae* suspended from baldrics and with beautifully detailed scabbards and Gundremmingen-type chapes. Other late iconographic evidence confirms the place of the *spatha* as the sword of the period.

OWNERSHIP

Roman soldiers, whether they were 1st-century AD auxiliary cavalrymen or 3rd-century AD legionaries, owned their *spathae*. Their weapons may have been supplied by the Roman Army and then deductions made from their subsequent pay, or they may have acquired them from private manufacturers. This is the reason why they were able to dedicate their weapons, a *spatha* being specifically cited in an inscription (*CIL* III, 14433,1; now lacking the name of its dedicant) of AD 226 from Silistra-Durostorum (Bulgaria). Because soldiers owned their swords, taking those belonging to others was deemed as theft in military law (*Digest* 49.16.3.14). Soldiers were also forbidden from discarding their weapons (*Digest* 49.16.14.1), so this implies that dedications and votive offerings can only have been made if the soldier concerned already had a replacement sword available to him. This would not have been the case if the weapon being dedicated was booty captured in a civil war – an extremely likely scenario – although it is always possible that a superior weapon acquired in this way may have rendered an existing *spatha* surplus to requirements and thus available for dedication in this way.

A careful account was kept to ensure that soldiers had the right equipment, as the letter of the auxiliary cavalry *decurio* Docilis to his commanding officer, listing equipment missing from the *ala Sebosiana* sometime before *c*.AD 105, shows (Tomlin 1998: 55–63). Surprising though it may seem, swords were included in his list. At the same time, javelins were also missing, so attrition in weaponry clearly occurred.

A few Roman *spatha* blades carry punched or scratched ownership inscriptions of the sort found on other items of military equipment, such as a sword from Illerup Ådal (Biborski & Ilkjaer 2006a: 309 finds group SAVL; 2006b: 192 & 217) with two *punctim* texts: 'Aureliu[s]' and '> PCRI+'. The first is the *nomen* of a Roman soldier in all likelihood, while the second includes a centurial sign meaning 'in the century of' and an indecipherable name. In all likelihood the latter weapon was booty taken from a Roman and dating to the 3rd century AD, following Caracalla's granting of universal citizenship, after which many newly enfranchised Roman soldiers took that emperor's *praenomen* and *nomen*, Marcus Aurelius. Interestingly, that blade (which also included an inlaid figure of Mars; see page 26) had broken at the top and had a new tang riveted in place. Another blade (Biborski & Ilkjaer 2006a: 309 finds group SANH; 2006b: 217) bore several *punctim* inscriptions, but all on the tang and in the main incomprehensible. Only three out of 53 swords from Illerup Ådal that bore stamps, inlay, or inscriptions carried such *punctim* lettering.

The rarity of such ownership inscriptions may possibly be due to the fact that the majority of surviving weapons were intended for export, but it may also be because such information was placed on the organic components of the handle, which are not often preserved in the archaeological record. One such example is a bone pommel from Ptuj (Slovenia), inscribed *Iustus optio cohortis II Aur(eliae) Dacorum* or '[Belonging to] Iustus, an *optio* in the *cohors II Aurelia Dacorum*'. The unit epithet *Aurelia* places this artefact into the second half of the 2nd century AD, during the reigns of Marcus Aurelius and Lucius Verus or Marcus' son Commodus, so it probably belonged to a *spatha*. Another factor may be that the corroded condition of many sword blades found within the boundaries of the Roman Empire mitigates against the survival of surface details such as *punctim* ownership inscriptions.

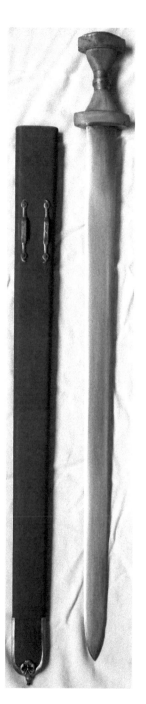

Illerup/Wyhl-type *spatha* reconstructed by Robert Wimmers. (Photo © R. Wimmers)

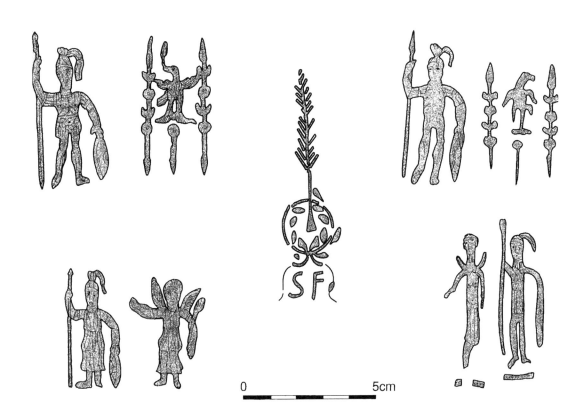

0   5cm

Inlaid figures in *spatha* blades.
(Drawings M.C. Bishop)

CARRIAGE

The historian Josephus usefully confirms that the early Principate *spatha* was worn on the right hip of the cavalryman:

> The horsemen have a long sword on their right sides and a long shaft in their hand; a shield also lies by them obliquely on one side of their horses, with three or more darts that are borne in their quiver, having broad points, and no smaller than spears. They have also helmets and breastplates, like those of all the infantry. And for those that are chosen to accompany the general, their armour in no way differs from that of the horsemen belonging to other troops. (Josephus, *Jewish War* 3.5.5)

Other evidence reveals how the early Principate *spatha* was suspended from a distinctive form of belt and is depicted on numerous cavalry tombstones as well as on the statue from Vachères (see page 9). The belt on this statue is shown fastening to the top pair of sword scabbard suspension rings, but also has an additional pair of straps passing to the lower suspension rings. In this, it differs from any representation of infantry sword suspension. The reason for this additional support may have been to help stabilize the sword scabbard while riding. By the early 2nd century AD, one particular type of cast, copper-alloy belt plate seems to have been specifically used by Roman cavalry in Britain (Bishop 2016a), with other types in use in the Rhineland (Jost 2007; Hoss 2009). Decorated with enamel inlay, only the buckle plates are ever found, suggesting that the rest of the belt was left unadorned. Attached to the leather with shanks moulded in one with the back of the object, such plates were usually in the region of 20mm in width and almost certainly occupied the full width of the belt. Unlike infantry equipped with the *gladius*, there is no evidence for the use of a baldric to carry the *spatha* at this early stage, probably because it would have been prone to movement in action, thus presenting the very real possibility that a sword could drift out of reach of a cavalryman at the very moment he needed it.

The method for drawing a cavalry sword suspended from a belt differed little from that of the *gladius* worn on the same side by infantrymen. The *spatha* could be easily drawn by inverting the right hand, with the thumb pointing down, then grasping the hand grip and drawing straight upwards. This naturally brought the sword into a raised position ready for a cutting blow if necessary.

At first, the scabbards of early Principate long swords were, unsurprisingly, developments of native weapons used by auxiliary cavalry. They employed the four-ring suspension system adopted from Celtiberian and Celtic models for the *gladius Hispaniensis*, generally fastened to the body of the scabbard with suspension bands. The copper-alloy scabbard included in the Corbridge Hoard is of this kind and presumably already an antique by the time of its deposition in the first half of the 2nd century AD.

By the time of the introduction of the Pompeii-type *spatha*, scabbards very closely reflected those of the shorter swords. Blade widths of Pompeii-type *spathae* and *gladii* were very similar, so the scabbards would likewise have been of the same width. Cavalry tombstones depict scabbards with edging strips, although when recovered by excavation, such U-sectioned binding, made of copper alloy, is indistinguishable from that of Pompeii-type *gladii*. Examination of the surviving locket plates and chapes similarly reveals no obvious differences in form – such as *spatha* plates perhaps being slightly taller in proportion to their width – to allow for the

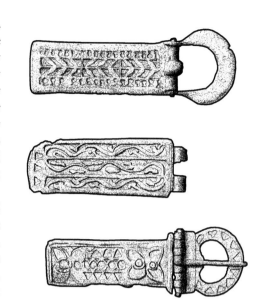

Cavalry belt plates from Caerleon (Gwent, Wales). (Drawings M.C. Bishop)

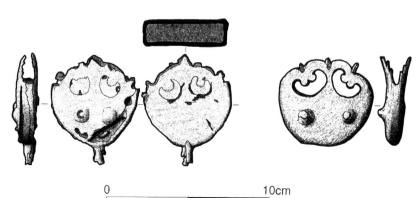

Unfinished copper-alloy casting of a scabbard chape from Corbridge (Northumberland, England; left and centre) together with a comparable finished example (right) from Stockstadt (Germany). (Drawings M.C. Bishop)

45

differentiation of long sword scabbards from short. Presumably they differed only in the length of their organic components (wooden laths wrapped in leather). It is conceivable that the subject matter on decorated scabbard plates may have in some way marked out the weapons of cavalrymen. To this end, a locket plate in a private collection (Miks 2007: 813, Taf.209, B100,37) which shows a cavalryman riding down a barbarian foe – a favourite theme on cavalry tombstones – may be relevant. Similarly, an embossed locket plate from Ptuj (Miks 2007: 861, Taf.207, B230,2) depicts the Dioscuri, the twin (half-brother) horsemen Castor and Pollux, another favoured theme for the decoration of cavalry equipment. However, there is no reason why locket plates (or chapes) decorated with other mythological scenes, particularly those involving Mars, could not also be used by cavalry. All of this suggests that Pompeii-type *spatha* scabbards, like those of the shorter *gladii*, consisted of a rectangular locket plate, triangular chape and an organic, parallel-sided sheath.

Coinciding with the introduction of the *spatha* into infantry units, there came a radical change in the manner of suspension of the sword. The waist belt was phased out and a new, broad baldric which tapered

A scabbard runner depicted on a member of a Sarmatian delegation on a cast of Scene C on Trajan's Column. (Photo © M.C. Bishop)

46

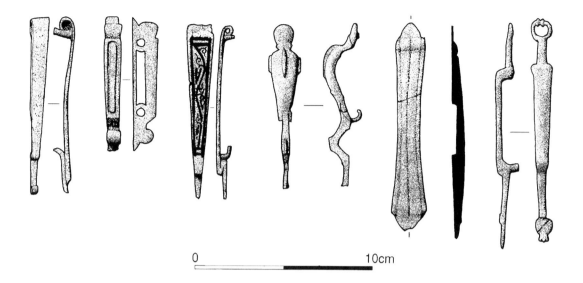

0 10cm

Examples of scabbard runners.
(Drawings M.C. Bishop)

was introduced. Moreover, the side on which the sword was worn changed too, moving to the left hip for all wearers, regardless of whether they were infantry or cavalry. At the same time, suspension loops on sword scabbards were replaced by a single, central 'scabbard runner' (also known in the literature as a 'scabbard slide'). Scabbard runners of this type are depicted on barbarian weapons on Trajan's Column, so it is likely that this form of suspension had trans-Danubian origins.

The earliest dated scabbard runner from within the Roman Empire comes from a burial mound at Čatalka (Bulgaria), a culturally mixed assemblage of material that included lamellar armour (not normally found within the Roman Empire at this time), a Roman cavalry face-mask helmet and a Chinese Han dynasty nephrite 'hydra' scabbard slide on a sword of Sarmatian origin with a Xiongnu-type Iranian chape (Gonthier *et al.* 2014)! This was an early herald for what was to come. Scabbard runners spread from the Far East, via the Eurasian steppe, and down into the Danube basin (Trousdale 1975). The Romans probably first encountered them en masse in the West in the second half of the 1st century AD, in their dealings with the Sarmatian Rhoxolani tribe in AD 68–69 (Tacitus, *Histories* 1.79). Under Marcus Aurelius, some 5,500 Sarmatian cavalry were incorporated into the Roman Army and sent to Britain (Dio, *Roman History* 71.16.2) so there were a variety of potential routes for the adoption of this system of suspension, all undoubtedly of Danubian origin.

It was originally thought that the narrow end of the baldric itself was wrapped around the scabbard and passed through the runner. Examples of scabbards still attached to baldrics from Illerup Ådal show how the leather was in fact secured by a pair of domed fungiform studs passing through the baldric, one stud on either side of the scabbard. The baldrics were also decorated with appliqué fittings, notably a disc or *phalera* that had a concealed loop to which the narrow end of the strap was attached, as well as a terminal plate with a hinged pendant at the broad end. There

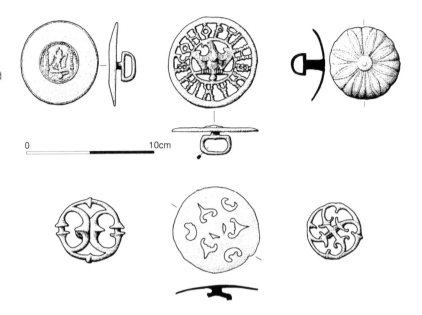

Baldric *phalerae* from Vimose (Denmark; top left), Carlisle (Cumbria, England; top centre), Saalburg (Germany; top right), Banasa (Morocco; bottom left and right) and Zugmantel (Germany; bottom centre). (Drawings M.C. Bishop)

are no obvious, clear distinctions between fittings from infantry, cavalry, or combined infantry and cavalry units, but excavated examples give an idea of the range of designs employed by troops during the latter half of the 2nd and most of the 3rd centuries AD.

Actual examples of *spatha* baldrics have been recovered from watery votive sites outside the Roman Empire in northern Germany and Denmark (Gräf 2009). Two leather baldrics – one made from cowhide and the other from goatskin – were retrieved from Thorsberg (Germany), while two more come from Vimose (Denmark). Comparison of the dimensions of

Baldric terminal plate and pendant sets from Silchester (Hampshire, England; top left), Zugmantel (Germany; top centre), Scole (Norfolk, England; top right), Saalburg (Germany; bottom left) and Zugmantel (bottom centre and right). (Drawings M.C. Bishop)

these with the *Price Edict* of Diocletian (section 10), which records two different widths (4 and 6 *digiti*, *c.*74mm and 111mm respectively) for *zona alba*, seems to equate to such baldrics.

Roman baldric *phalerae* from Vimose (Denmark). (Photo CC-BY-SA, John Lee, National Museum of Denmark)

DECORATION AND DISPLAY

Pattern welding has already been discussed as a technique of manufacture (see page 24) and it was mentioned that there is debate as to whether this was a purely decorative technique or whether it was thought to impart some additional strength to the weapon, making it resistant to bending.

In the letter from Theodoric cited above, he describes rather poetically what is almost certainly pattern welding as *videntur crispari posse vermiculis* 'revealing small, wriggling worms' inside the fullers, noting 'where there is such variety playing together in the shadow, the brilliant metal seemed to be interwoven with a variety of colours' (Cassiodorus, *Letters* 5.1.1, trans. author). It cannot be discounted that swords were prized as much for their appearance – perhaps even more so – than for their practical qualities.

Spathae of the 2nd and 3rd centuries AD also saw another innovation in the decoration of the blades themselves (Biborski 1994). The technique of inlaying a different metal into the steel of the blade (damascening) included depictions of sets of three standards (with a central eagle), palm branches, and Mars and Victory, through to what are, in effect, derivative stick figures. Interestingly, these decorative designs were intended to be

49

viewed with the pommel at the bottom and the blade tip at the top, presumably so that they were visible to the owner when the sword was held in front of the face or out in front.

The replacement of the short *gladius* with the longer *spatha* for infantry also brought about a radical change in the style of scabbard decoration. The earlier openwork and embossed sheet-metal plates covering the organic core fell from favour and a much simpler style of sheath became the norm.

As has already been mentioned, the means of suspension was now reduced to just one fitting on the scabbard itself, the so-called scabbard runner, although the range of types in use during the 2nd and 3rd centuries AD show that a taste for variation was still present. Unlike the earlier method of mounting, with articulated rings attached to either side of the scabbard, a single scabbard runner was mounted on the front face of the organic sheath (usually with a pair of lugs) and did not actually bear any direct weight, because the end of the baldric was wrapped around the sheath and was then just held in place by the runner and prevented from slipping upwards or downwards. Some modern reconstructions have employed additional binding around the top and bottom of the scabbard runner to secure them in place, but examples found *in situ* do not support this practice. The decoration of these scabbard runners could range from extremely simple and functional loops, right up to cast items imitating the shape of a leaping dolphin. Materials used included forged iron (usually for simpler designs), cast copper alloy, carved bone and ivory, and even wood.

The other principal scabbard fitting was the chape, reinforcing the tip of the sheath. Chapes were produced in the same range of materials as the scabbard runners and included peltate and box forms in the 2nd and early 3rd centuries AD, with disc chapes becoming popular in the later 3rd and 4th centuries AD.

The body of the scabbard was made out of wooden laths (front and back) and scientific analysis of 108 examples from Illerup Ådal showed that over half were fashioned from lime wood (Biborski & Ilkjaer 2006a: 351–53), like that from De Meern. Other woods used included poplar, alder, willow and birch. Some, but by no means all, scabbards were bound at the edges with metal guttering. The De Meern sword lacked edging but a significant number of those from Illerup Ådal incorporated binding and these included iron, copper alloy and even silver. However, just as some handle assemblies seem to have been locally produced, the same seems true of scabbards, so what is true of these northern finds need not necessarily have applied to finds within the Roman Empire (the Lyon and Canterbury burials, for example, lacked any such edging).

The complete Straubing/Nydam-type *spatha* found in waterlogged conditions still in its sheath at De Meern afforded an opportunity to examine a well-preserved organic scabbard in some detail. It was fashioned from two sheets of lime wood covered (and held together) by leather, with a peltate chape and scabbard runner made of iron (Aarts 2012: 235). An unusual and rather interesting scabbard was found together with the Khisfine sword in Syria. Although it superficially resembled a standard 3rd-

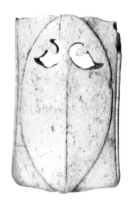

century AD *spatha* sheath, it was in fact made entirely out of ivory (Gogräfe and Chehadé 1999). Whereas conventional scabbards of the period – such as the De Meern example – were manufactured from wood and leather, with metal suspension runners and chapes, these components were integral to the Khisfine sheath. Ivory was extremely valuable in the Roman period; Diocletian's *Price Edict* valued it at one-fortieth of the price of silver by weight, so this was no ordinary piece.

The means of producing metallic scabbard components changed with time, partly as a result of fashion, but also due to technological developments. During the early Principate period, metal scabbard fittings were usually made out of sheet metal, often stamped and embossed, but still requiring sheet to be made (by beating out or perhaps even rolling) in the first instance. At the time, the usual method of casting copper alloys was by what is known as the lost wax (*cire perdue*) technique, which required a wax model to be made, clay shaped around that to form the mould, and then the molten metal poured in, melting the wax. The fact that the mould had to be broken to get the object out meant that the method was not conducive to mass production. The adoption of the two-part mould in the 2nd century AD meant that original objects could be used to form the two halves of the mould, into which the metal could be poured. The mould could be re-used and accurate copies of the original produced in substantial numbers (depending upon the life of the mould). A failed casting of a copper-alloy peltate chape from Corbridge shows that there was still an element of finishing needed after an object had been cast, but that was true of any complex casting.

CARE AND MAINTENANCE

Whether *gladius* or *spatha*, a sword needed essentially the same sort of care and maintenance to ensure both its longevity and efficacy. The orator Fronto's comment on the advisability of keeping a sword clean (*On Eloquence* 1.16) is obviously as true for a long sword as it was for the

Three examples of scabbard chapes of the later 2nd/early 3rd century AD in copper alloy and bone. (Photos P. Gross © Arachne)

short and the means to achieve this the same. Hones and whetstones continue to be found on Roman military sites from the period when the *spatha* took over from the *gladius* and are, as might be expected, indistinguishable from earlier examples. In his letter of thanks for the gift of some swords, Theodoric marvels at their finish and notes that it is almost as if they were too good to be finished with *pulvis* (literally 'dust', but also used of pumice).

Similarly, because organic materials were still favoured for the hilt, it must be assumed that whatever treatment these were subject to on *gladii* would not have changed with the advent of the *spatha*. The use of copper-alloy inlay on some later Principate blades would have required careful cleaning to avoid bimetallic corrosion, but the fact that blades did not normally break in this region suggests that this was diligently and successfully practised.

Intriguingly, the presence of a *punctim* (presumably ownership) inscription on the tang of a sword from Illerup Ådal raises the possibility that the sword-handle assemblies may occasionally have been dismantled, although the need to remove the peened-over top nut to do this would have ensured that this was only undertaken when absolutely necessary.

TRAINING

The historian Arrian, himself a friend of the Emperor Hadrian and commander of the army based in Cappadocia, wrote an account in Greek (his favoured language) of the elaborate cavalry training and display manoeuvres which he called the *hippika gymnasia*. This complex series of mounted evolutions required accuracy in the casting of javelins as much as skill in controlling the horse, but one part of the exercise involved the use of the sword: 'Then they draw their *spathae* and strike as often as they can, either reaching for a fleeing enemy or killing a fallen one, or directing blows to either side as they advance' (Arrian, *Tēchne Taktikē* 43.3, trans. the author). Here the cavalrymen were mimicking striking at their enemies and it was presumably the fluency, frequency and efficacy with which they demonstrated this that gained them kudos in the *hippika gymnasia*. Moreover, killing a fallen foe required the cavalryman to show his skill as a horseman by leaning down out of his saddle. The four-horned saddle, which provided a firm and secure seat for the rider and more than made up for the fact that there were no stirrups available, enabled him to perform such a manoeuvre.

Vegetius' passages on training infantry in his *De Re Militari* were compiled from older authors at a time when cavalry was a dominant arm and foot soldiers had, he felt, been unjustly neglected. The type of training he advocated, known as the *armatura*, involved indulging in sword play against a *palus*, a man-sized stake set into the ground, against which the soldier practised with a double-weight wooden sword.

The ancients, as is recorded in the books, trained recruits in this way. They wove rounded shields of wicker like basketry, in such a way that the frame should be double the weight of a battle shield. And likewise they gave the recruits wooden weapons, also double weight, in place of swords. And next they were trained at the stakes, not only in the morning, but also in the afternoon. For the use of stakes is particularly advantageous not only for soldiers but also for gladiators. And neither arena nor field ever proved a man invincible in arms, unless he was carefully taught training at the stake. However, single stakes were fastened in the ground by each recruit, in such a way that they did not wobble and protruded for six feet [1.56m]. The recruit practised against this stake with the wicker shield and singlestick as though with a sword and shield against an enemy; so, he might aim for the head or face, then he is threatened from the sides, then he strained to cut down at the hams and shins; he retreated, attacked, leaped in, as if the enemy were present; he assaulted the stake forcefully, fighting skilfully. In doing this, care was taken that the recruit rose up in this way in order to wound, but did not lay himself open to a blow anywhere. (Vegetius, *DRM* 1.11)

Evidently, without practice to strengthen the wrist (one of the things training against the stake could build), problems could ensue when wielding the sword:

Martinus, alarmed by this threat, and seeing the imminent danger to his life, drew his sword and attacked Paulus. However, because his hand was weak he was unable to wound him mortally and then plunged his drawn sword into his own side. Thus, with this unseemly type of death, a most just man died. (Ammianus, *Res Gestae* 14.5.8)

The incorporation of sword drill into the *hippika gymnasia* certainly looks like a formalization of the regular *armatura* that cavalrymen too would have been required to perform every day. Taken together, then, these sources provide a glimpse into how sword drill was practised with the long sword for both infantry and cavalry.

The implication of Vegetius' description of the *armatura* is, of course, that this was no longer done in the Late Roman Empire. There is thus no guarantee that the *spatha* was trained with, or even used, in the same way throughout its service with the Roman Army. However, understanding the manner of its use is pivotal to explaining why Roman infantry came to adopt what had been, until the mid-2nd century AD, a purely cavalry weapon.

The debate that is embedded within the text of Vegetius (which he unquestionably reflects in various passages, to the point of seemingly contradicting himself) – whether to use the tip or the edge of the blade in hand-to-hand combat – might on first sight seem to be irrelevant to the use of the long sword. However, it should always be remembered that the longest examples of the *gladius Hispaniensis* (Bishop 2016a: 31) were longer than the shortest specimens of the *spatha*, so viewing the *spatha* as a weapon designed purely for cutting or chopping may be an overly simplistic interpretation. Certainly, the point was as prominent on

Straubing/Nydam-type *spatha* reconstructed by Robert Wimmers. (Photo © R. Wimmers)

Pompeii-type *spathae* (like those from Newstead) as it was on Pompeii-type short swords, implying its use for thrusting. In a passage that probably derives from the general Iulius Frontinus, Vegetius notes of infantry undergoing training that 'They are very frequently occupied in striking with wooden singlesticks in place of swords, stabbing and cutting for many days until they sweat' (Vegetius, *DRM* 3.4).

INTO BATTLE

The obvious conclusion from the passage in Arrian cited above is that, after basic weapons training and once he could master his horse, a cavalryman was regularly instructed in the use of the sword as a secondary weapon to his javelins. Accordingly, the convention was to show cavalrymen of the period wielding shafted weapons on their tombstones, only Insus being depicted with his sword drawn (and apparently just used). Arrian, in a document setting out a battle plan in case of invasion by the steppe nomad Alani, described how, if his force was flanked, the cavalry on the wings (if disadvantaged) were to fight with swords and axes, rather than with shafted weapons, which they might not be in a position to use (Arrian, *Ektaxis kata Alanon* 31).

It is interesting (but not necessarily significant) that the Roman emperor Valerian is depicted on the Paris Cameo as wielding his *spatha* as if for a slashing blow in his mounted encounter with the Sassanid Persian king Shapur. As representations go, Valerian's sword is no better or worse than that on Insus' tombstone, but the hilt assembly is obviously intended to be that of a standard sword, rather than the familiar eagle pommel so often found associated with emperors' statues.

Direct evidence of the *spatha* in action is rare, but the remains of a battle fought underground in a countermine at Dura-Europos in Syria may offer grim testimony to its use (James 2004: 34–37). At some point

Legionaries breaking into the city of Dura-Europos (opposite)

During the Parthian Wars of Lucius Verus in the middle of the 2nd century AD, the Roman Army laid siege to the Parthian-held city of Dura-Europos on the west bank of the Euphrates in what is now Syria. Demolishing the Hellenistic walls fashioned from large gypsum blocks by means of both continued artillery bombardment and battering rams, the Romans were finally able to gain access to the northern part of the city in AD 164. Led by their adventurous general Avidius Cassius, legionaries of *legio III Gallica* charge in through two large gaps created on either side of Tower 22, while archers and slingers outside provide covering volleys of missiles to keep the defenders on the walls and towers pinned down. The legionaries are now equipped with *spathae*, and both Lauriacum/Hromówka and Straubing/Nydam types can be seen in use, both cutting and stabbing, their scabbards equipped with peltate chapes. One or two *spathae*, broken earlier in the campaign, having been fashioned into *semispathae* by forging new tips for them, are being used to stab in the manner of the short *gladii* of earlier years.

in the middle of the 3rd century AD, a Sassanid Persian army lay siege to the garrison town of Dura-Europos on the west bank of the Euphrates. Using mines dug under the walls (unsuccessfully, it appears) and a ramp, they were able to take the city, but not before the defenders, including Roman soldiers, put up a bitter fight. One of their mines was intercepted by a countermine dug by the Romans, and within it archaeologists found the remains of an underground battle, where the Romans were fighting with *spathae*.

Such a vignette is unusual, but archaeological evidence for the use of the *spatha* can supply both the weapons themselves and the fittings for their scabbards and baldrics from many locations across the Roman Empire. Finds from the battle of Abritus (Radoslavona *et al.* 2011), fought near modern-day Razgrad in Bulgaria in AD 251, were recovered under less-than-ideal circumstances, but nevertheless included *spathae* and associated fittings. Three published examples (how many have been lost is unknown) measured 680mm, 850mm and 725mm in length, with widths ranging from 35mm to 45mm and fall within the parameters for the Straubing/Nydam type of the sword. A number of circular scabbard chapes also come from the site.

One indication of the use of *spathae* in battle is thought to be the frequency with which *semispathae* are found, most of which have been made from cut-down *spathae*. Converting a broken *spatha* into a short sword was an efficient way to recycle an otherwise useless blade, as well as satisfy the persistent liking for short swords (Bishop 2016a: 28), but it may also reflect the way in which the long sword was used in battle. Roman swords were not designed for Hollywood-style blade-on-blade fencing and clashing blades in this way may well have seen a proportion of them break. Describing combat with the Persians, the sounds Ammianus invoked included 'clashing armed men, groaning casualties, snorting horses, and ringing swords [*tinnitus ferri*]' (Ammianus, *Res Gestae* 25.3.12). During the battle of Strasbourg in AD 357, he likewise noted that 'in hand-to-hand conflict, sword struck sword and tore open armour' (Ammianus, *Res Gestae* 16.12.46). In his description of the same battle, he provided an echo of Polybius' old gibe against the long sword: 'our soldiers, now slashing at the backs of the fugitives, and finding their swords so battered that they were insufficient to wound, used the enemy's own javelins, and so slew them' (Ammianus, *Res Gestae* 16.12.52).

As had been the case with the *gladius*, the reason Roman infantry normally avoided fencing was because they instinctively fought with the shield as a complementary weapon to the *spatha*, as well as a parrying defence (this is why they trained with a double-weight shield). When Julian found himself confronted by a couple of determined Persian soldiers, 'he encountered them with his shield raised, and protecting himself with that, and fighting with great and noble courage, he ran one of them through the body, while his guards killed the other with repeated blows' (Ammianus, *Res Gestae* 24.4.4).

Parrying with the shield against an enemy too expansive in their style of hand-to-hand combat could also provide opportunities to strike: '... covering themselves with their shields as the *mirmillones* do, with their

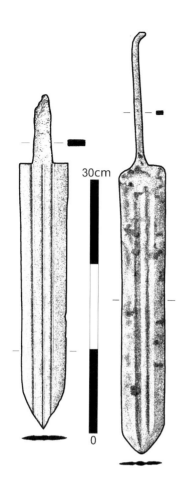

30cm

0

drawn swords wounded their antagonists in the sides, which their too-vehement impetuosity left unprotected' (Ammianus, *Res Gestae* 16.12.49). This comparison with the style of combat practised by *mirmillones* not only harks back to the origins of the *armatura* as a means of training both soldiers and gladiators, but also recalls the stab/cut debate reflected by Vegetius.

Examination of the sword blades found at Illerup Ådal and Ejsbøl reveals a range of types of attrition to blades in addition to (what is assumed to be) the ritual 'killing' of the weapons by bending and folding. Nicks in the edges (and even the top) of a blade, or even scratches on its surface, at various locations may be additional evidence of such complex ritual behaviour (Biborski & Ilkjaer 2006a: 343–44, Abb.171), but some at least could also originate as damage sustained in battle (Dr D. Sim pers. comm.). If any of this damage was indeed sustained in combat, it could well be that the Germanic owners of the blade chose to fight with the swords in a different way to the Romans, perhaps even parrying with the blade rather than the shield. Certainly, nicks to the edge near the hilt and near the point could have two different causes (parrying with the blade in the former case, striking with the tip in the latter), which speaks against the Roman method of fighting. Even if the damage is ritual in origin, it could reflect a real and very familiar model of damage to combat weapons. Ultimately, this is all speculation, but interesting nevertheless.

There is something of a lack of skeletal remains of Rome's foes from the Principate and Dominate periods which could be examined to determine the nature of the wounds received from Roman *spathae* (James 2009: 42–43). Literary accounts (for all their biases and caveats), and even damaged swords, are one matter, but they scarcely bear comparison with actual human remains that can be scientifically analysed. This does not mean skeletal remains will never be found – the remains from the Republican Roman attack on Valencia in 75 BC are a gruesome testament to this – just that this material has yet to be recovered under controlled archaeological conditions in sufficient quantities to be informative. However, there is evidence from Roman cemeteries of wounds that may have been caused by *spatha*-like swords (see page 61).

Why, then, did the Roman Army come to favour the *spatha* over the short sword? There are tantalizing hints that the favoured style of infantry combat changed during the Principate. The late Peter Connolly, citing the way in which Roman helmet neck guards became deeper throughout the 1st century AD, argued that a more upright combat stance had developed and that the helmets reflected this (Connolly 1991). By the 3rd century AD, helmet neck guards were so deep that an upright stance was forced upon the soldier, and it has been suggested that this may be why the infantrymen in the countermine at Dura-Europos were helmetless: they had no choice but to crouch in the confined space available and the large neck guards on their helmets would have made this impossible. Connolly's suggestion has inevitably had its critics, particularly among re-enactors who have doubted the Roman soldier's ability to sustain the early crouched stance advocated. Nevertheless, the idea provides one model for the way in which infantry combat changed in the Roman Army.

Ejsbøl-type *spatha* from Medinet Habu (Egypt). (Photo © Royal Ontario Museum)

An alternative explanation requires an argument *ex silentio*, so is inevitably destined to be less intellectually satisfactory. It depends upon interpreting the writings of Vegetius in their strictest sense. The method he used to compose his *De Re Militaris*, evident from careful textual analysis, was essentially to crib the work of earlier Roman writers on military affairs. His discussion of tactical spacings in the battle line, together with the equivocal advocacy of different ways of using a sword – to stab (*punctim*) or to cut (*caesim*) – can be seen as evidence for the fact that such details were unknown in his time. In other words, the way in which Roman soldiers fought in hand-to-hand combat had changed, not so much in their stance, as Connolly suggested, but in the tactical spacing each man used on the battlefield. This would almost certainly have affected the way the soldier employed both his sword and shield, but would this have been a result of using a longer sword, or was the longer blade adopted because this change was already occurring and the short sword was becoming inadequate?

Unsurprisingly, the available evidence cannot answer any of these questions definitively and, once again – beyond the basic fact that the change to the *spatha* occurred – all that remains is speculation and hypotheses. Perhaps it was as simple as the need for weaponry to evolve in the face of new enemies that drove these changes (James 2011: 183–88).

DISTRIBUTION

When studying ancient weapons, the evidence is all too often incomplete to the point of opacity, but sometimes it simply fails altogether. A case in point is the obvious dichotomy between the Straubing/Nydam and Lauriacum/Hromówka types of *spatha*, which persisted throughout the 2nd and 3rd centuries AD and so was quite clearly deliberate. The reason behind the dichotomy is not mentioned in the literary sources, however, nor is the representational evidence of any help. Unfortunately, studying the distribution of the two types of *spatha* within the Roman Empire provides no obvious answer.

The use of the *spatha* was by no means confined to the Roman Army. By far the largest number of surviving Roman long swords come from the northern votive deposits in Germany and Denmark, but there are also some examples from burials belonging to the Przeworsk Culture (usually thought to be associated with the Vandals) in what is now Poland, and one of the type-swords comes from a burial at Hromówka in Ukraine. While some of these undoubtedly entered the archaeological record as booty, there were complex issues at work dictating the circumstances of deposition, undoubtedly fed by the export of Roman weaponry throughout Northern Europe. At its simplest, swords that were captured from the Romans were being dedicated in these deposits, but it is equally possible that weapons supplied to one faction or tribe were being captured by other Germanic groups and then deposited. Many of these swords seem to have been supplied as just blades so that handles could be fitted locally, allowing indigenous tastes (especially marked in pommel shapes) to be satisfied. This explains why many of the manufacturers' stamps were placed on the tang, where they would no longer be visible after the addition of a handle.

There is no way of knowing what proportion of the total exports of swords ended up in votive deposits or burials, let alone what proportion of those have subsequently been recovered. It is entirely possible that there were more *spathae* in use within the Roman Empire at any given time than existed outside it, but that the survival of weapons in the archaeological record has been skewed precisely because of those northern votive deposits.

Who was conducting this trade? A funerary altar from Mainz in Germany was set up on behalf of Gaius Gentilius Victor, a veteran of *legio XXII Primigenia* (which was based there in the late 2nd century AD), whose trade was declared to be *negotiator gladiarius*. This 'trader in swords' (using *gladius* in its generic sense) set aside 8,000 sesterces in his will for the altar, which was dedicated to the Emperor Commodus (sole emperor from AD 180 to 192) and to Fortuna Redux, a goddess whose special area of interest was safe return after a long journey. That altar cost more than twice a contemporary legionary's annual salary, so the arms trade was apparently both lucrative and, given the invocation of Fortuna Redux, hazardous.

There does not seem to have been a reciprocal trade in weaponry beyond the eastern borders of the Roman Empire, not least because this was where Rome's major enemies (the Parthians and Sassanid Persians) were to be found in the 2nd and 3rd centuries AD. If anything, eastern influence was travelling westwards, although not to a significant degree and not necessarily directly. As discussed above, the mound at Čatalka containing a high-status burial included military equipment from beyond the frontiers, such as a suit of lamellar armour (not found in the West at this date) and a Chinese Han dynasty nephrite 'hydra' scabbard slide.

Recognition of the existence of this arms trade north of the Roman Empire begs the question of whether swords were manufactured specifically to supply it. Producing weaponry to supply a potential enemy may seem somewhat strange, but it has to be remembered that the sword did not normally play the same role in Germanic society as it did with the Romans. Tacitus makes it plain that most Germanic tribes favoured fighting with spears, so swords of the kinds that come from the watery contexts of Northern Europe were deposited precisely because they were viewed as high-status items. Clearly, the Romans believed that these swords would not be used against them in any meaningful numbers.

There may ultimately have been unpleasant (but not entirely unforeseeable) consequences of this arms trade, however. The battle of the Willows in AD 377, for instance, saw Roman forces opposing Goths whose use of the sword had devastating consequences:

And while the whole battlefield was covered with corpses, some were lying among them who were mortally wounded, and cherished a vain hope of life; some were smitten with a bullet from a sling or pierced with arrows tipped with iron; the heads of others were split through

Votive altar from Mainz (Germany) set up by the *negotiator gladiarius* (trader in swords) Gentilius Victor, a former soldier of *legio XXII Primigenia*. (Photo © bpk-Bildagentur)

mid-forehead and crown with swords and hung down on both shoulders, a most horrible sight. (Ammianus, *Res Gestae* 31.7.14)

The sort of wounds described, and even the preference for the use of the sword, makes it likely that these were *spathae* that were being used against the Romans, as Davidson (1962: 197) suggested.

In fact, a small number of Late Roman burials from northern Pannonia in the Danube basin have produced clear signs of sword cuts to the head (Merczi 2009: 166–67). Out of 545 skeletons examined from four cemeteries, only three adult male skulls (from Nyergesújfalu, Esztergom and Visegrád-Diós, all in Hungary) displayed such trauma, so it is a tiny percentage overall and thus statistically insignificant, but interesting nevertheless. All three skulls had been struck from the front with blows by right-handed assailants. Examination of skeletons in other cemeteries revealed a higher incidence of sword wounds. At Tác, also in Hungary, 11.7 per cent of males and 1.4 per cent of children had received sword wounds (Merczi 2009: 181). In contrast, skeletons in the city cemetery at Pécs (Hungary) in what was south-eastern Pannonia displayed no comparable sword wounds, implying that the more northerly victims of the sword resulted from frontier unrest. The swords taking their toll on the inhabitants of Pannonia were most likely to have been *spathae* and may have been the ultimate consequence of two centuries of trading such swords. Indeed, Ammianus noted how important the sword had become to the Germanic tribe of the Quadi, when 'drawing their swords, which they worship as deities, they swore to remain faithful' (*Res Gestae* 17.12.21).

Likewise, examination of burials from Zadar in Croatia (Novak 2013) revealed wounds which can be interpreted as sword cuts, including – in Grave 378B – a (non-fatal) blow to the head of an individual from above, probably dealt by a *spatha* wielded from on horseback, followed by a fatal cut across the skull. Others exhibit wounds were indicative of a blow to the femur, perhaps to sever the femoral artery.

CONCLUSIONS

It is a common misconception that the *spatha* was adopted as a result of the increasing Germanic ethnicity of Roman troops under the Principate. This is to put the cart before the horse, however. It is clear that swords were not as popular as the thrusting spear with Germanic tribes in the 1st and 2nd centuries AD, a fact Tacitus emphasizes. In the 2nd and 3rd centuries AD, troops from the Danube basin certainly came to dominate the Roman Army, but these were drawn from peoples with a long history of participation in the Roman imperial project. Only when Germanic tribes started to threaten and even invade the frontiers of the Roman Empire during the 3rd and 4th centuries AD did assimilation become a reality, long after the *spatha* had been adopted as the sidearm of choice for legionaries and auxiliaries. Arguably, the Romans gave the Germans the long sword, rather than the other way round.

The move away from the short sword to the longer blade of the *spatha* during the 2nd century AD thus reflected two continuing Roman strands of thinking about swords. The longer *gladius Hispaniensis* had been the perfect weapon for both infantry and cavalry but, when replaced by the shorter and lighter Mainz-type blades, it in turn necessitated the development of longer swords specifically for cavalry. The subsequent adoption of the *spatha* by infantry as well as cavalry thus brought the story of the Roman sword full circle. Such oscillations can only have been due to the demand for a multi-purpose weapon that provided the best of both worlds: sufficient reach for both infantry and cavalry, without its mass being overly irksome. In other words, function was dictating fashion. The Straubing/Nydam and Lauriacum/Hromówka types of *spatha* were therefore direct inheritors of a tradition begun by the *gladius Hispaniensis*, four centuries earlier. Indeed, they were destined to have an even longer-lasting effect.

IMPACT
The sword that defended an empire

In a modern, throwaway society, it is easy to forget just how important recycling was in the ancient world: 'And He shall judge among the nations, and shall rebuke many people: and they shall beat their swords into ploughshares, and their spears into pruning hooks: nation shall not lift up sword against nation, neither shall they learn war any more' (Isaiah 2:4). These lofty sentiments serve as a reminder that most Roman swords have been lost forever and those that do survive do so because of unusual circumstances. The ease with which a blacksmith could re-forge ferrous objects is often underestimated and it was as true of swords as any other artefact. A broken *spatha* from Vindolanda seems to have been discarded while in the process of having its blade reworked in just this way. It should always be remembered that, if weapons survive in the archaeological record, it is because somebody took the trouble to place them there, by whatever means.

USING THE *SPATHA*

While the *gladius Hispaniensis* and its successors were weapons that could be used equally well for stabbing and chopping, the *spatha* was from its very beginnings a cutting blade. This is not surprising, given its origins (in Roman service, at least) as a cavalry weapon, where a cutting stroke was far less likely to run the risk of leading to the loss of a weapon which became stuck during a thrusting blow. It was also well suited to a slicing blow in passing, reflecting the early Principate auxiliary cavalry's principal role of mopping up a fleeing enemy after they had been broken.

As is the case with the *gladius*, we lack first-hand Roman accounts of using the *spatha*, nor are there any technical manuals on the finer points of its use. Again, with only a few near-contemporary general texts, seldom written by specialists, all assessments must be based on the weapons themselves. Many *spathae* are damaged in some way and most are now extremely fragile. Although experimental archaeology can be profitably employed in reconstructing a sword and evaluating its efficacy, the results from such experiments must be treated with caution. Experimental archaeology is only capable of showing what might have been possible, not what definitely happened, and this is sometimes forgotten. For the *spatha*, as with the *gladius*, much depends upon the accuracy of the reproduction for assessing qualities that might today be taken for granted: the more accurate a reproduction is, the better it can be assessed. If the modern swordsmith simplifies or 'improves' a design (and many do), then that will invariably detract from the value of the experiment.

Thanks to well-preserved finds from sites like Illerup Ådal, we are quite well informed about the weights of *spathae* (Biborski & Ilkjaer 2006a: 323–34). Classified into five categories of blade weight, ranging from under 0.5kg ('very light') to more than 1kg ('very heavy'), the Illerup Ådal finds show just how much variation there was among these swords. In addition to the weight of the blades themselves, the handles had to be factored in. As Biborski and Ilkjaer point out, the handle assembly on the same type of sword could account for between 12 per cent and 30 per cent of its entire weight, depending upon whether it was a simple wooden assembly (0.146kg from a total weight of 0.956kg) or a decorative example of ivory adorned with silver and gold (0.263kg from 0.898kg). Thus two swords of similar overall weight might be balanced very differently.

Hilt assembly of pommel, handle and hand guard made from bone (Miks A160), from Dorchester (Dorset, England).
(Photo © J.C.N. Coulston)

The handle provided the soldier with the crucial element of control over the *spatha* which, like the handle of the *gladius*, was extremely ergonomically designed. The hand grip was nearly always organic and frequently made from a sawn length of cow metapodial bone, although horse bone was also occasionally used, along with ivory and wood. Among *gladii*, the hand grip was usually between 75mm and 94mm long (averaging 84mm, close to the average width of the modern male hand), but there are fewer indisputable *spatha* hand grips from Roman contexts for such certainty, the bulk of those surviving coming from northern votive deposits where the swords may well have been fitted with the preferred handle locally. Ribbed forms of hand grips continued in use after the 1st century AD, but the facetted form was much rarer on *spathae* than they had been for *gladii*, although they were by no means unknown. In truth, while facetting undoubtedly aided control of the sword, in fact it was not essential, because hand grips continued to be oval by virtue of the fact that most were still made from cow metapodials which naturally tended towards ovoid in cross-section and would thus resist rotation in the hand.

A variety of types of hand grip beyond just the ribbed form are known from the later Principate period, as can be seen from those still attached to swords. There are even more isolated examples which must have belonged to *spathae*, showing that spiral-carving had come back into fashion, but all types combine decoration with functionality. A Straubing/

Straubing/Nydam sword from Straubing (Miks A700) with damascened brass 'stick figure'. (Photo Fotowerbung Bernhard/ Straubing © Gäubodenmuseum)

Nydam sword found in a temple at Calès-Mézin in France (Miks A91) still retained its bone hand grip with geometric designs incised into its surface. An unusual hand grip from Dura-Europos was near-square in cross-section and its smooth surface was decorated with small teardrop-shaped protrusions which provided the necessary purchase. Other, similar examples are known from the German frontier.

On Roman *spathae* (as opposed to exports), the top of the hand guard and base of the pommel were convex, as on the *gladius*, so that the hand was squeezed onto the handle (this form of hilt was still in use on the late-3rd-century AD Köln sword). The thumb rested against the top surface of the hand guard to ensure a firm grip. The shaped pommel and hand guard therefore produced an extremely secure grip, allowing the soldier to feel that the sword was a true extension of his arm. Again, as with the *gladius*, the variation in lengths of surviving hand grips suggests that swords were to some degree fitted to the individual. Too small a hand grip would tend to crush the user's hand, while too large a grip would reduce the precision of the soldier's control of the weapon, for lack of contact with the hand guard and pommel would tend to cause the weapon to pivot about the hand when it was swung.

An organic hand guard on a *gladius* could be reinforced with copper-alloy sheet and such basal plates could also be found on some (but by no means all) later Principate *spathae*, such as the Lyon sword, only more substantial and in this case decorated with openwork designs. The provision of enhanced protection demonstrates that blades (whether sword, spear or dagger) sliding up the sword towards the handle were anticipated as a hazard.

A limited range of types of blow were available to the soldier on horseback or on foot. The shield ruled out any sort of backhand cut for either. Stabbing (*punctim*) could be used by the infantryman and would have been appreciated for its economy of effort, potential for dealing fatal blows, and the protection it afforded to the user. Vegetius noted that a wound two *unciae* (49mm) deep was sufficient to kill (Vegetius, *DRM* 1.12). Although economical, stabbing had its limitations, particularly with the shorter *gladius* or *semispatha*. The stance adopted in Roman hand-to-hand combat, with the left foot and shield advanced and the right foot and sword held back, meant that the effective range of the weapon was limited. Indeed, as the limit of the reach of the individual was approached during a stabbing blow, so the force that could be brought to bear would have decreased dramatically. The greater length of the *spatha* helped alleviate this problem, but it was by stepping forward with the right leg to deliver a blow that this situation was most easily resolved. The maximum range then came from the sword shoulder being forward of the shielded side. Judging the distance for an effective blow was as important for the *spatha* as for shorter swords, and it is here that practice at the stake had such an important role to play. It served to familiarize the soldier with the best distance from an opponent during combat that provided a compromise between effective reach and minimum risk.

The most obvious blow with a long sword like the *spatha* was the downward cut (*caesim*) and this was clearly going to be favoured by

Roman cavalrymen. Despite Vegetius' observation that this type of attack exposed the side of the infantryman delivering it, it had the advantage of being aided by gravity as well as not unbalancing the user sideways so could also be used on foot. If necessary, with the arm raised, the pommel of the sword could be brought down rapidly to strike with the top nut, should an opponent get too close. Oblique and lateral cuts were theoretically possible, but ran the risk of placing the swordsman off balance, while the lateral cut could also end up impacting the man's own shield! An upward cut was unlikely, because it was against gravity and not capable of carrying much force, but would undoubtedly have been employed if no alternative presented itself.

The overall mass of the sword depends upon the amount of metal in the blade and tang, as well as the materials used: any combination of wood, bone or ivory with additional brass components and perhaps even a foil coating. Its balance then in turn depends upon the distribution of those components. Modern reconstructions suggest that, while the *gladius* gradually became lighter from the *Hispaniensis* through to the Pompeii type, the *spatha* matched and even surpassed the earliest *gladii* in weight. Here, naturally, much depends upon the quality of the reconstructions. Distal taper – which will have served to move the centre of gravity away from the point and towards the handle – is evident on some blades, but by no means all. Detailed measurements of blade thickness are lacking for *spathae*, even in modern studies. Corrosion is inevitably a major factor preventing accurate measurements being taken, however.

The assessment of the 'feel' of a sword such as the *spatha* remains as subjective now as it did to the Romans. It is not even possible to be certain that what feels well balanced to a modern swordsman would necessarily have met with the approval of a Roman infantryman or cavalryman. What is certain is that the longer blades meant that the centre of balance would be shifted further towards the point than was the case for the short sword. To a soldier who had never fought with a short sword, however, such a consideration was probably irrelevant: they coped with what they knew.

Experimental archaeology can go some way to providing credible performance data. However, there is always a danger that what it supplies is an approximation of what weapons similar to the *spatha* (but which might vary in slight – but perhaps important – details) could achieve. Unprotected flesh would always be vulnerable to the *spatha*, but the situation is less clear once other materials are brought into play, most notably (but not solely) metallic armour, such as scale, mail and plate, particularly when that protection was used with any sort of padded backing, such as the *thoracomachus* described by the anonymous author of the *De Rebus Bellicis*.

Ultimately, it is important to recall that the Roman cavalryman, like his infantry counterpart, trained with a double-weight substitute so that virtually any true sword was going to feel lighter. As two comparatively recent advocates of singlestick combat suggested, 'it is not a bad thing to accustom yourself to using the heaviest sticks in the gymnasium. This will

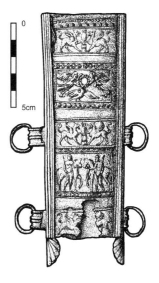

Scabbard fittings from *spathae* are ubiquitous in the areas formerly within the Roman Empire. Perhaps most notable is the decorated scabbard locket plate in the Ptuj Regional Museum (Miks B230; Slovenia) near the former site of the legionary base of Poetovio. (Drawing M.C. Bishop)

strengthen your wrist, and when in a competition you get hold of a light ash-plant, you will be all the quicker for your practice with a heavier stick' (Allanson-Winn & Phillipps-Wolley 1905: 60).

PSYCHOLOGICAL AND PHYSICAL IMPACT

The psychological impact of the *spatha* in the early Principate period was doubtless enhanced by the circumstance under which it was usually encountered – when fleeing from the Romans. This can perhaps be summed up best by the image of Insus on his tombstone: spears may have been for killing, but swords were needed for head-taking. Originally a practice described by Diodorus Siculus (*Historical Library* 5.21.5) and Strabo (*Geographica* 4.4.5) when discussing the Gauls, head-taking seems to have been a tradition their cavalry brought with them into their service with the Roman Army. Auxiliaries are even shown presenting severed heads to the emperor on Trajan's Column (Scenes XXIV and LXXII), but the message there is less clear than that on the relief showing Insus. After all, the Romans were not averse to lopping off the heads of political enemies, although they did draw the line at keeping the severed heads with them as trophies. Were the Trajan Column's sculptors depicting the barbaric brutality of non-citizen, auxiliary soldiers to contrast them with the civilized citizen legionaries? Or was this a simple demonstration of their efficacy and loyalty to their emperor? The fact that the man who ultimately took the Dacian king Decebalus – Tiberius Claudius Maximus – gave Trajan his foe's head as evidence of his death indicates that, whatever the moral standpoint of those sculptors, the reality was quite clear: the taking of heads, while not widespread, was certainly practised without compunction in the Roman Army. Skulls found outside the ditch of the legionary fortress of Colchester-Camulodunum (Essex, England) and the auxiliary fort of Vindolanda tell the same grim tale of intimidation and brutality, while Trajan's Column depicts heads on stakes mounted on fortifications in Dacia (Scene LVI).

WORDS AND WEAPONRY

The origin of the Latin word *spatha* lies with the Greek σπάθη (which transliterates as *spathe*), a flat implement used in weaving to tighten the weft, and the term can be found in the work of the playwright Aeschylus (525–456 BC). As early as the 6th century BC, however, the Greek poet Alcaeus was evidently using the word to refer to a sword. The Greek historian Diodorus Siculus echoed this in the 1st century BC, noting of the Celts 'For swords, they use a long and broad weapon called the *spatha* [σπάθη], which they hang across their right thigh by iron or brazen chains' (*Bib. Hist.* 5.30). For the Roman philosopher Seneca, however, writing in Latin in the 1st century AD, a *spatha* was indeed a batten used in weaving (*Epistulae* 14.90). His contemporary, the agricultural writer Columella, used the term to denote a spatula (*De re rustica* 22.22). Thus, there seems little doubt that the Roman weapon was named from the Greek implement and σπάθη was not a contemporary Greek transliteration of the Latin word *spatha*.

The word *spatha* was first used by Tacitus to mean a sword when he was writing the *Annals* (a work which was probably published under Hadrian), but the decurion Docilis, in his list of equipment missing from the *ala Sebosiana*, referred to cavalrymen lacking a *gladium* (sic) *institutum* or regulation sword (*gladius* probably being used here generically for sword). Also writing under Hadrian, Arrian (*Tēchne taktikē* 4.7) refers to the Roman cavalry sword (σπάθη) as long and flat. It therefore looks as if the adoption of the term *spatha* for the Roman cavalry sword is no earlier than the reign of Hadrian (AD 117–138) and that it was a direct borrowing from the Greek, which is somehow appropriate for an emperor nicknamed '*graeculus*' ('the Greekling').

Despite this, many of the terms familiar from the language of the short sword (*mucro* and *ensis*, together with *ferrum*) continued to be used as euphemisms for the weapon until, by the time Ammianus Marcellinus was writing, he never actually used the word *spatha* for a sword.

By the time Isidore of Seville came to compile his *Etymologies* in the late 6th or early 7th centuries AD, he does not appear to have had a clue as to the genuine origin of the word, although his comments do at least reflect the chief characteristics of the blade: 'It is said *spatha* comes from the Greek for passion, since παθεον is 'to suffer' in Greek, and we use *patior* [I am suffering] and *patitur* [he is suffering]. Others insist that it is *spata* in Latin, from the fact that it is *spatiosa* or broad and long' (Isidore, *Etym.* 18.6.4). The term '*spathion*' continues to be found in Byzantine texts, such as those of Nikephoros Phokas and Nikephoros Ouranos, while the court title of '*spatharios*' survived into the 10th century AD.

The Latin word *spatha* went on to form the root of derivative words meaning 'sword' in the Romance languages, where it can be detected in Italian (*spada*), Spanish (*espada*), Portuguese (*espada*), Basque (*ezpata*), Catalan (*espasa*), French (*épée*, from the Old French *espee*) and Romanian (*spadă*), so in that respect at least the *spatha* was far more influential than the *gladius*. Even English preserves a memory of it in the Latin loan-word, spatula ('little sword'), although 'sword' is Germanic in origin.

As an interesting aside, in AD 226, an inscription (*CIL* III, 14433,1) from Silistra uses the term *spata* when listing some items of equipment. Rather than *spata* being a spelling mistake, it is likely that this is indicative of the way the word was actually pronounced in the Roman Army (*th* and *t* were much closer in Latin than in English: Allen 1965: 27), which in turn explains the later derivatives of the word.

Silver brooch of the 2nd/3rd century AD depicting a *spatha* scabbard with runner and peltate chape. The item is hollow so originally may have held a model sword.
(Photo P. Gross © Arachne)

POLITICS AND THE *SPATHA*

Because an emperor's personal bodyguard during much of the 1st century AD were German horsemen, the *Germani corporis custodes*

(so-called 'Batavi'), it is likely that he found himself surrounded by men wielding *spathae*, just as the Praetorian Guard carried the shorter *gladii*. So when Caligula's assassins felled him with short swords in AD 41, they in turn would have been killed by the bodyguards' long swords.

An instance of auxiliary cavalrymen using the sword for political assassination occurs during the civil war of AD 69, and it shows just the sort of flexibility in choice of weaponry that might be expected. The legionary commander in Africa decided to get rid of the proconsul, Piso:

> he despatched some cavalry to kill Piso. They rode over at full speed and broke into the proconsul's house in the dim light of early dawn, with their drawn swords in their hands. Many of them did not know Piso, for the legate had selected some Moorish and Carthaginian auxiliaries to perform the deed. Near the proconsul's bedroom, they came upon a slave and asked him who he was and where to find Piso. The slave nobly lied, replying, 'I am he,' and was instantly cut down. (Tacitus, *Histories* 4.49)

Little had changed when Ursicinus came to replace the allegedly mutinous general Silvanus under Constantius II and sent in assassins to remove him: 'They killed the guards and entered the palace, and so, having dragged Silvanus out of a small chapel where, in fright, he had taken refuge on his way to a secret meeting devoted to the ceremonies of the Christian worship, they slew him with repeated blows from their swords' (Ammianus, *Res Gestae* 15.5.31).

DERIVATIVES

Unlike the *gladius*, the *spatha* was to prove extremely influential in the early medieval period, not only in the eastern Byzantine Empire, but also among the northern peoples of what Romans would once have referred to as Barbaricum. The *spatha* was still to be found within the former Roman Empire. The sword buried with the Sutton Hoo warrior (possibly the Anglian King Raedwald) was a *spatha*; similarly, the sword of the legendary sub-Roman British warlord, Artorius (if it and he ever existed) would have been a *spatha*. Given the profuse and profound medieval additions to the myth of (by then) Arthur, there is no way to know whether the legends of either the 'sword in the stone' or Excalibur were in any way related to the Roman *spatha* or its derivatives, but weapons from this period occasionally survive.

There is perhaps one memory embedded in the whole medieval tradition of the Arthurian tale, and that is the deposition in and retrieval of swords from watery resting places. Everybody remembers Excalibur being hurled back into the lake by Sir Bedivere when Arthur cannot bring himself to do so (Oakeshott 1991: 3–4), and it is not hard to see a folk memory of the dedication of swords in water in this (whether it is correct is another matter). Taking swords that have been put beyond use also

Early 6th century AD Anglo-Saxon sword from Buckland (Kent, England). (Photo © The Trustees of the British Museum)

occurs, however: a 7th-century AD Viking, Skeggi of Midfirth, dug an old sword out of a burial mound precisely so he could continue to use it (Oakeshott in Peirce 2002: 6).

The direct influence of imports of Roman *spathae* on Northern European tribes is plain to see in finds from the early medieval period, not least because the peoples who migrated west to the south and east of Britain brought *spathae* with them. A predilection for including swords among weapons burials provides a useful record of the status of the *spatha* among its new users. Hilts certainly differed from their Roman predecessors, as did scabbards to a lesser extent, but the ancestry of the blades remained clear.

Pattern-welded blades were still highly prized, but now the technology was understood and blades no longer needed to be imported. It is a fairly straightforward process for a competent smith to 'reverse-engineer' pattern welding and, once understood, it is easily passed along. We know this to be true because modern smiths' ability to forge pattern-welded blades harks back to the work of John Anstee in the 1960s, when he used known examples of original blades as an aid to understanding the process (Davidson 1962: 217–24). This helps explain why pattern welding is sporadically found among the Etruscans in the 7th century BC and Iron Age peoples in the 3rd century BC, before the Romans adopted it for the *spatha* in the 2nd century AD.

The Angles, Saxons and Jutes, who arrived in Britain in the Late and sub-Roman periods, originated in precisely the area of Northern Europe whence Roman weapons exports are best known. Sword blades that show the clear influence of Roman technology abound in the Saxon period and

The *spatha* and scabbard from the Sutton Hoo ship burial (Suffolk, England) as reconstructed by Róbert Môc. (Photo © Bohumil Šálek)

30cm

0

Unprovenanced Viking swords of the late 9th century AD from the Musée de l'Armée in Paris (France) (above) and the 10th century in the National Museum, Copenhagen (Denmark) (opposite). (Drawings M.C. Bishop)

it is unsurprising that one such should have been buried with the elite individual, probably a king, at Sutton Hoo (Suffolk, England). Indeed, the rarity of swords in grave finds suggests that they had become a sidearm of elite warriors (Davidson 1962: 9).

A sword found in the remains of a Roman villa hypocaust at Feltwell (Norfolk, England) has been dated to the early 5th century AD and assumed to be Anglian in origin. It was deposited still in its organic scabbard with a U-shaped chape and ferrous scabbard runner, and it was believed by its excavators to have been deliberately concealed. The blade, which X-rays show to have been etched but not pattern welded, was 628mm long and 48mm wide with a lenticular cross-section, the whole weapon surviving to 736mm.

Burial 1800 at Snape (Suffolk, England) contained a sword which has been dated to the turn of the 6th/7th centuries AD, but its origins are still clear. With an overall length of 920mm, this sword blade was 790mm long and 50mm wide.

A weapon from Ely Fields Cemetery in Cambridgeshire provided insights into the way that a pattern-welded blade was formed in Anglo-Saxon England. The cemetery, part of which was bulldozed to make way for a wartime airfield, was loosely dated between the 5th and 8th centuries AD. This sword was 864mm long in total, of which 775mm was the blade, 44mm and 3mm thick, and the twisted core was 15mm wide. A break revealed the cross-section, showing how 43 separate strips had been interwoven to form the blade.

Arguably the best-known of the Anglo-Saxon swords is that from what is probably a royal burial (often identified as Raedwald) in Mound 1 at Sutton Hoo. The sword, which was lifted intact, had an overall length of 851mm, of which 720mm was the pattern-welded blade, which tapered from a maximum width of 64mm.

In modern-day Germany, the town of Krefeld-Gellep is renowned not only as the site of a major cavalry battle (and associated horse burials) from the time of the Batavian Revolt of AD 69/70, but also for being the location of a large Frankish cemetery. Unsurprisingly, this, like the Anglo-Saxon cemeteries in England, has produced examples of *spatha*-type swords. One example that has undergone detailed study is dated to the 6th or 7th centuries AD. The weapon is 860mm in overall length, the blade comprising 740mm of that, and although 55mm wide and an average of 5.4mm thick for most of its length, it tapers to the point over the last third. The sword was weighed at 0.76kg, although the effects of corrosion mean that figure is not an accurate reflection of its original weight. Scientific examination of the weapon determined that it had been damascened but not pattern welded.

The Langobardi were a Germanic tribe whose burials in the Danube basin (such as Grave 44 at Szentendre in Hungary) during the first half of the 6th century AD show their warriors interred with their *spathae* on their left-hand side. Langobard swords in burials from northern Italy demonstrate how they brought those swords with them when they settled in that region in the late 6th and early 7th centuries AD. A sword found in a warrior's assemblage from Fornovo San Giovanni in the Italian province of Bergamo had a central fuller and was pattern welded (Christie 1991: 12 and Fig. 7). The military laws of Aistulf from the middle of the 8th century AD required that farmers and free men should possess a sword, shield and archery equipment, so for them a *spatha* was less of a high-status item than it was for the Saxons or Vikings.

It is clear from the documentary sources that swords among many Germanic peoples were reserved for elite members of society in the post-Roman era, most of them warriors fighting with spear and shield. This reflected the pattern found in most tribes described earlier in Tacitus' *Germania*, so it is hardly surprising, but – in its own way – it marks a change in the way that the *spatha* was used.

The interchange of ideas in Northern Europe seems to have spread into Scandinavia (*Beowulf*, it will be remembered, was a poem about Geatish warriors that was written in Old English). Viking swords, which still bore comparison with Roman originals right through to the 11th century AD, had the same common origin of those from northern Germany and demonstrate just how far Roman swords originally travelled. Indeed, archaeological finds reveal how swords and scabbards in what is now Norway were showing Roman influence as early as the 1st century AD, with an evident local interest in the *gladius Hispaniensis*.

As happened within the Roman Empire, the shorter blades fell from favour in Northern Europe, to be replaced by the longer, *spatha* type. Between the 7th and the 11th centuries AD, five distinctive blade forms have been identified. The first form (7th–8th centuries) was 700–800mm in length with parallel edges and short tips. Some examples had fullers and these blades were usually pattern welded. The second form (8th–10th centuries) was slightly longer (740–830mm) and with marked taper on the blade but not the fuller. Some were pattern welded, but some of those that were not bore Ulfberht inscriptions (Oakeshott in Peirce 2002: 7–9). The same inscriptions (the purpose of which is unclear) could be found on some of the third type of blade, of similar length and with a similar taper, but with a tapering fuller. These date from the latter part of 8th century into the first half of the 10th century. The fourth type of blade, which could also be pattern welded, dates from the middle of the 10th century to the middle of the 11th century and was generally shorter (630–760mm) and narrower than the earlier forms, with both blade and fuller tapered. The fifth and final blade form belongs in the period from the middle of the 10th century through to the end of the 11th century and is much longer (generally in the range 840–910mm), once again with taper in the blade and (sometimes) the fuller.

There is a separate classification of Viking swords according to their hilt types (Jones in Peirce 2002: 16–22), but this owes little to their Roman antecedents so is of little concern here. What this typology of blade forms does, however, is remind us of the longevity of the *spatha* type of sword – there are examples of Roman swords that are closely comparable in size and form to all of these main types of Viking blade. Not only form but

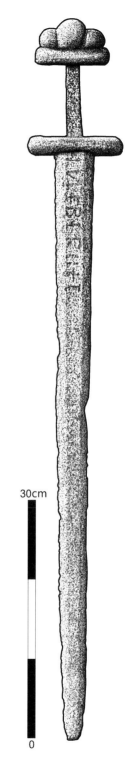

30cm

0

also the technology (pattern welding and inlay) were unquestionably derived from Roman traditions.

Although the forms were recognizably the same, the manner in which Viking swords were used seems to have been very different from the Romans. The historian Saxo Grammaticus (2.56) describes the combat style of the period, trading blows and pausing between bouts. Cutting blows were clearly favoured, to judge from literary accounts (Davidson 1962: 196–97).

In the East, Byzantine swords retained similar blades to their Roman predecessors but very different hilt assemblies and scabbards. Unfortunately, comparatively few actual examples of such swords are known, most of the studies on the subject necessarily relying upon literary and, most particularly, iconographic depictions (of which there are many). A weapon from Galovo in Bulgaria (8th–9th centuries AD) is thus key to linking the typology of hilt types with a surviving example of these later *spathae*. It has a lenticular cross-section, lacking either a midrib or fullers, and is parallel-edged with a short, rounded point. The 890mm-long weapon retains its copper-alloy hand guard but lacks a handle or pommel. The hand guard, effectively a nascent cross guard, has two straight arms terminating in a simple trefoil design with a smaller cylinder above and a larger cylinder below (Rabovyanov 2011). Other examples are known from Bulgaria, and such hilts can be found depicted in later 11th-century AD mosaics from Chios and Daphni (both in Greece), thus confirming the persistence of the *spatha* beyond the early medieval period.

MODERN RECONSTRUCTIONS

Although the *spatha* nowadays lacks the iconic status of its shorter sibling, the *gladius*, there are plenty of reconstructions to be seen of both Roman and later weapons. The re-enactment market ensures that there are mass-produced examples of early Principate cavalry *spathae* available to buy off the shelf. That same source also provides copies of weapons from the later Principate and even Dominate periods. More impressive perhaps are those swords produced by specialist craftsmen, often to commission (including those for museums), and which tend to be more closely based on the archaeological evidence than cheaper, mass-produced offerings. A third category of reconstruction covers those weapons produced by re-enactment groups themselves where, once again, a high value is placed upon accuracy to the original archaeological source material. These too may sometimes be commissioned for museum displays.

The criteria upon which a reproduction sword may be judged do not just come down to how similar it looks to the weapon being copied. A comparison between a modern replica of a sword from Illerup Ådal and the actual weapon upon which it was based revealed that the modern reconstruction was in fact *c*.22 per cent heavier (Biborski & Ilkjaer 2006a: 334).

Pompeii-type *spatha* scabbard reconstructed by the Ermine Street Guard; it accompanies the *spatha* shown on the front cover. The scabbard locket plate is a replica of the example found at Ptuj (Slovenia).
(Photo © M.C. Bishop)

CONCLUSION

Ultimately, the *spatha* proved to be an extremely wise compromise on the part of the Roman Army. The key to the *spatha*'s success undoubtedly lay in its versatility. Whether mass produced to equip auxiliary cavalry fighting from horseback in the 1st century AD, legionary infantry both cutting and stabbing in the 2nd and 3rd centuries AD, or Saxon and Viking warriors trading blows between elite opponents, the *spatha* just seemed to be right.

Given that the *spatha* survived into at least the 10th century AD, the question of what succeeded this thousand-year-old weapon is an interesting one. There had been a gradual tendency for *spatha* blades to increase in size in the post-Roman period in the West, and this continued throughout the medieval period to the point where the two-handed sword became a reality. The practice of pattern welding died out at the end of the Viking era, however (Jones in Peirce 2002: 145), and was lost within the area of the former Roman Empire and its neighbours until revived by modern blacksmiths, led by John Anstee. In short, the *spatha* provided a direct link between Iron Age long swords through to some of the finest bladed weapons of the early medieval period (Oakeshott 1991: 1).

As for survivors, many examples of the *spatha* type of sword and its associated scabbard fittings can be found throughout the museums of Europe. Early Principate *spathae* from Newstead can be seen in the National Museums of Scotland in Edinburgh. The Rottweil *spatha* is on display in the Dominikanermuseum in Rottweil (Germany) itself. By far the largest collections of *spathae* come from the northern votive deposits already mentioned. Although most of these either have no grip assemblies or have been modified with local forms of hilt, the blades and tangs are either Roman or Roman-influenced. Material from the Danish sites such as Illerup Ådal and Vimose can be viewed in the National Museum of Denmark in Copenhagen and the Moesgaard Museum in Højberg, while artefacts from Nydam and Thorsberg are displayed at Schloss Gottorf in Schleswig.

GLOSSARY

alveus   *see* fuller.

baldric   strap for suspending a scabbard from one shoulder.

blade   forged in one with the tang; that part of the weapon not enclosed within the handle.

caesim   a cutting or chopping blow with a blade.

chape   the bottom of the scabbard, where the point of the sheathed weapon rested.

cross guard   bar below the hand grip and above the blade.

damascening   a process for decorating the surface of the blade by inlaying another metal.

distal taper   thinning of a blade from tang to tip.

forge welding   heating separate pieces of ferrous metal and forging them together into one piece; also known as fire welding.

frame scabbard   edged with guttering and held together with lateral bands that included suspension bands.

frog   button for attaching a scabbard to a belt.

fuller   a longitudinal corrugation of the blade that both strengthens it laterally and lightens it. Sometimes (incorrectly) referred to as a 'blood channel'.

guttering   U-sectioned strips that bound the edge of a scabbard.

hand grip   made of organic material (wood, bone or ivory) and shaped to be easy to hold.

hand guard   expansion below the hand grip that protects the hand of the user; made of organic material (wood, bone or ivory).

hand guard plate   metal plate beneath the hand guard designed to protect it from blows.

handle   the hand guard plate, hand guard, hand grip and pommel assembly, fastened onto the tang by means of the peen block.

hollow ground   whereby (in order to lighten it) a blade is given a convex surface between edge and midrib by means of grinding.

locket plate   metal plate on the front and at the top of the scabbard (just below the mouth), often decorated.

midrib   the thickest part of the blade when viewed in cross-section.

mouth   the uppermost part of the scabbard.

mouth plate   the very top of the scabbard that opposed the hand guard plate when a sword was sheathed.

pattern welding   forge welding ferrous strips together and twisting them to form a blade.

peen block   moulded copper-alloy knob used to fasten the handle components onto the tang; so called because the tip of the tang is peened over the block.

phalera   disc attached to baldric with loop to the rear, used for fastening it.

piling   forge welding ferrous strips (often of differing degrees of hardness) together longitudinally to form a blade.

point   that part of the blade which narrows to the tip.

pommel   swollen counterweight above the hand grip to provide balance for the sword; made of organic material (wood, bone or ivory).

quillons   medieval metal hand guard.

punctim   a stabbing blow with a blade; also a technique for making ownership inscriptions in dots with a punch.

scabbard   metal and organic sheath designed to contain and protect the blade when not in use.

scabbard runner   attachment to the front face of the scabbard, through which the baldric passed; also known as a scabbard slide.

shoulder   the abrupt expansion from the tang to the blade.

singlestick   wooden practice sword.

suspension band   metal band that attached the suspension rings to the scabbard. The *spatha* invariably had two suspension bands, each with one suspension ring on either side.

suspension ring   the point of attachment for the scabbard to a belt or baldric, fixed to the scabbard by means of a suspension band.

tang   forged in one with the blade, that part of the weapon covered by the handle.

terminal knob   a cast, bulbous fitting that united the guttering at the bottom of the chape.

tip   the end of the blade.

top nut   brass cap over (or acting as) the peen block.

BIBLIOGRAPHY

Ancient sources

Ammianus Marcellinus, *The History*. 1939–50 Loeb ed., trans. J.C. Rolfe. Available at https://tinyurl.com/yb8npc (accessed 9 January 2019).

Arrian, *Ektaxis kata Alanon*. Trans. S. van Dorst. Available at https://tinyurl.com/ydckr4sp (accessed 9 January 2019).

Arrian, *Tēchne taktikē*. Available at https://tinyurl.com/y8vzxewq (accessed 8 January 2019).

Cassiodorus, *Letters*. 1886 trans. T. Hodgkin. Available at https://tinyurl.com/yd9d34h6 (accessed 8 January 2019).

Cassius Dio, *Roman History*. 1914–27 Loeb ed., trans. E. Cary. Available at https://tinyurl.com/52t38g (accessed 8 January 2019).

Digest. 1932 Central Trust Company ed., trans. S.P. Scott. Available at https://tinyurl.com/ybc66j2j (accessed 8 January 2019).

Diodorus Siculus, *Historical Library*. 1952 trans. C.H. Oldfather. Available at https://tinyurl.com/ycs8kr9p (accessed 8 January 2019).

Fronto, *Correspondence* (includes *On Eloquence*). 1919 Loeb ed., trans. C.R. Haines. Available at https://tinyurl.com/y8okzhvb (accessed 8 January 2019).

Isidore of Seville, *Etymologies*. 2005 trans. P. Throop. Available at https://tinyurl.com/ycozcv5r (accessed 8 January 2019).

Justinus, *Epitome of Pompeius Trogus' Philippic Histories*. 1853 trans. J.S. Watson. Available at https://tinyurl.com/ydcty2bt (accessed 8 January 2019).

Philon, *Belopoeica* in *Mechanicae syntaxis*. 1919 trans. H. Diels & E. Schramm. Available at https://tinyurl.com/y9jc2nn9 (accessed 8 January 2019).

Plutarch, *Parallel Lives* (including *Camillus*). 1923 Loeb ed., trans. B. Perrin. Available at https://tinyurl.com/5ufwsd (accessed 9 January 2019).

Polybius, *Histories*. 1922–27 Loeb ed., trans. W.R. Paton. Available at https://tinyurl.com/298bsf (accessed 9 January 2019).

Saxo Grammaticus, *Gesta Danorum*. 1905, trans. O. Elton. Available at https://tinyurl.com/y6mmeu4n (accessed 18 July 2019).

Strabo, *Geographica*. 1917–32 Loeb ed., trans. H.L. Jones. Available at https://tinyurl.com/2khpq4 (accessed 8 January 2019).

Tacitus, *Annals and Histories*. 1925–37 Loeb ed., trans. J. Jackson. Available at https://tinyurl.com/8jpv49 (accessed 9 January 2019).

Tacitus, *Germania*. 1876, trans. A.J. Church and W.J. Brodribb. Available at https://tinyurl.com/y9zpgq7s (accessed 9 January 2019).

Vegetius, *De Re Militari*. 1885 Lang. Available at https://tinyurl.com/ybvq5ypu (accessed 9 January 2019).

Modern sources

Aarts, A.C. (2012). *Scherven, schepen en schoeiingen*. LR62. Archeologisch onderzoek in een fossiele rivierbedding. Utrecht: Bakels.

Aleksić, M. (2010). 'Some typological features of Byzantine spatha [*sic*]', *Recueil des travaux de l'Institut d'études byzantines* 47: 121–36.

Allanson-Winn, R.G. & Phillipps-Wolley, C. (1905). *Broad-sword and Single-stick*. London: Bell & Sons.

Allason-Jones, L. & Bishop, M.C. (1988). *Excavations at Roman Corbridge: the Hoard*, London: English Heritage.

Allen, W.S. (1965). *Vox Latina*, Cambridge: Cambridge University Press.

Biborski, M. (1993). 'Die Schwerter des 1. und 2. Jahrhunderts n. Chr. aus dem römischen Imperium und dem Barbaricum', *Specimina Nova* 9: 91–130.

Biborski, M. (1994). 'Römische Schwerter mit Verzierung in Form von figürlichen Darstellungen und symbolischen Zeichen', in Carnap-Bornheim, C. von, ed., *Beiträge zu römischer und barbarischer Bewaffnung in den ersten vier nachchristlichen Jahrhunderten*. Lublin/Marburg: 107–35.

Biborski, M. & Ilkjaer, J. (2006a). *Illerup Ådal. Die Schwerter: Textband*, vol. 11. Århus: Jysk Arkæologisk Selskab.

Biborski, M. & Ilkjaer, J. (2006b). *Illerup Ådal. Die Schwerter: Katalog, Tafeln und Fundlisten*, vol. 12. Århus: Jysk Arkæologisk Selskab.

Biborski, M., Kaczanowski, P., Kedzierski, Z. & Stepinski, J. (1985). 'Ergebnisse der metallographischen Untersuchungen von römischen Schwertern aus dem Vindonissa-Museum Brugg und dem Römermuseum Augst', *Gesellschaft pro Vindonissa. Jahresbericht*: 45–80.

Birch, T. (2013). 'Does pattern-welding make Anglo-Saxon swords stronger?', in Dungworth, D. & Doonan, R.C.P., eds, *Accidental and Experimental Archaeometallurgy*, London: Historical Metallurgy Society, 127–34.

Bishop, M.C. (2016a). *The Gladius. The Roman Short Sword*. Weapon 51. Oxford: Osprey.

Bishop, M.C. (2016b). 'Roman cavalry belt fittings from Britain?', *Arma* 15: 14–16.

Bishop, M.C. & Coulston, J.C.N. (2006). *Roman Military Equipment from the Punic Wars to the Fall of Rome*. Oxford: Oxbow Books.

Braat, W.C. (1967). 'Römische Schwerter und Dolche im Rijksmuseum van Oudheden', *Oudheidkundige Mededelingen* 48: 56–61.

Bruce-Mitford, R. (1978). *The Sutton Hoo Ship Burial: Volume II. Arms, Armour and Regalia*. London: British Museum Press.

Busch, A.W. & Schalles, H.-J., eds (2009). *Waffen in Aktion: Akten der 16. Internationalen Roman Military Equipment Conference (ROMEC). Xanten, 13.–16. uni 2007*, Xantener Berichte 16. Mainz: von Zabern.

Christie, N. (1991). 'Longobard Weaponry and Warfare, A.D. 1–800', *Journal of Roman Military Equipment Studies* 2, 1–26.

Connolly, P. (1991). 'The Roman fighting technique deduced from armour and weaponry', in Maxfield, V.A. & Dobson, M.J., eds, *Roman Frontier Studies 1989*. Oxford: Oxbow Books: 358–63.

Davidson, H.E. (1962). *The Sword in Anglo-Saxon England*. Woodbridge: Boydell.

Engelhardt, C. (1865). *Nydam mosefund, 1859–1863*. Copenhagen.

Engelhardt, C. (1869). *Vimose fundet*. Copenhagen.

Gogräfe, R. & Chehadé, J. (1999). 'Die Waffen führenden Gräber aus Chisphin im Golan', *Journal of Roman Military Equipment Studies* 10: 73–80.

Gonthier, É., Kostov, R.I. & Strack, E. (2014). 'A Han-dated "hydra"-type nephrite scabbard slide found in Chatalka (Bulgaria): the earliest and most distant example of Chinese nephrite distribution in Europe', *ArkéoLog* 65: 5–12.

Gräf, J. (2009). 'Die Schwertgurte aus dem Thorsberger Moor', in Busch & Schalles 2009: 131–36.

Hoss, S. (2009). 'The military belts of the *equites*', in Busch & Schalles 2009: 313–22.

James, S. (2004). *The Excavations at Dura-Europos: Conducted by Yale University and the French Academy of Inscriptions and Letters. VII, The Arms and Armour and Other Military Equipment*. London: British Museum Press.

James, S. (2009). 'The point of the sword: what Roman-era weapons could do to bodies – and why they often didn't', in Busch & Schalles 2009: 41–54.

James, S. (2011). *Rome and the Sword: How Warriors and Weapons Shaped Roman History*. London & New York, NY: Thames & Hudson.

Jost, C.A. (2007). 'Vorbericht zu den Ausgrabungen 2002–2004 im Limeskastell Niederberg bei Koblenz', in Thiel, A., ed., *Forschungen zur Funktion des Limes 2*, Stuttgart, pp. 48–55.

Lang, J. (1988). 'Study of the metallography of some Roman Swords', *Britannia* 19: 199–216.

Merczi, M. (2009). 'Verletzungen an spätrömischen Schädeln aus Nordost-Pannonien', in Busch & Schalles 2009: 165–82.

Miks, C. (2007). *Studien zur römischen Schwertbewaffnung in der Kaiserzeit*. 2 vols. Rahden: Verlag Marie Leidorf.

Miks, C. (2015). 'Eine späteisenzeitliche *spatha* in des Kaisers Diensten? Zur Wechselwirkung der Schwerttraditionen am Beginn der Kaiserzeit', in P. Henrich *et al.*, eds, *Non solum ... sed etiam. Festschrift für Thomas Fischer zum 65. Geburtstag*, Leidorf: Rahden/Westf., 285–99.

Nicodemi, W., Mapelli, C., Venturini, R. & Riva, R. (2005). 'Metallurgical investigations on two sword blades of 7th and 3rd century B.C. found in Central Italy', *ISIJ International* 45:9: 1358–67.

Novak, M. (2013). 'Tavern brawls, banditry and battles – weapon injuries in Roman Iader', in Sanader *et al.*, eds, *Proceedings of the XVIIth Roman Military Equipment Conference. Weapons and Military Equipment in a Funerary Context*, Zagreb: Arheološki muzej u Zagrebu, 347–56.

Oakeshott, E. (1991). *Records of the Medieval Sword*. Woodbridge: Boydell.

Ortisi, S. (2015). *Militärische Ausrüstung und Pferdegeschirr aus den Vesuvstädten*, Palilia 29. Wiesbaden: Dr Ludwig Reichert Verlag.

Peirce, I. (2002). *Swords of the Viking Age*. Woodbridge: Boydell.

Pleiner, R. (1993). *The Celtic Sword*. Oxford: Clarendon Press.

Rabovyanov, D. (2011). 'Early medieval sword guards from Bulgaria', *Archaeologia Bulgarica* 15(2): 73–86.

Radoslavova, G., Dzanev, G. & Nikolov, N. (2011). 'The battle at Abritus in AD 251: written sources, archaeological and numismatic data', *Archaeologia Bulgarica* 15(3): 23–49.

Rald, U. (1994). 'The Roman swords from Danish bog finds', *Journal of Roman Military Equipment Studies* 5: 227–41.

Rapin, A. (2001). 'Des épées romaines dans la collection d'Alise-Sainte-Reine', *Gladius* 21: 31–56.

Tomlin, R. (1998). 'Roman manuscripts from Carlisle: the ink-written tablets', *Britannia* 29: 31–84.

Trousdale, W. (1975). *The Long Sword and Scabbard Slide in Asia*. Smithsonian Contributions to Anthropology 17, Washington: Smithsonian.

Ulbert, G. (1974). 'Straubing und Nydam. Zu römischen Langschwertern der spaten Limeszeit', in Kossack, G. & Ulbert, G., eds, *Studien zur vor-und frühgeschichtlichen Archäologie*. Munich: Beck, pp. 197–216.

Williams, A. (2012). *The Sword and the Crucible: A History of the Metallurgy of European Swords*. Leiden: Brill.

Wuilleumier, M.P. (1950). 'La bataille de 197', *Gallia* 8: 146–48.